5.99

LOBBY CARDS

LOBBY CARDS
THE CLASSIC FILMS

THE MICHAEL HAWKS COLLECTION

Foreword by Joan Bennett

Text by Kathryn Leigh Scott

Pomegranate Press, Ltd. · Los Angeles · London

This is a Pomegranate Press, Ltd. book.

The Library of Congress Catalog Card Number is 87-061592.

ISBN: O-938817-11-6

NOTES ON THE COMPOSITION
Book Jacket Design: Tom Nikosey
Book Design: Nikosey Design / SteeleWorks Design
Photographic Reproduction: Ben Martin
Photographic Assistant: Byron Cohen
Research: Kathleen Resch

The text was typeset in Goudy Oldstyle Condensed by Marchese Graphics Incorporated, Los Angeles; and was printed and bound in Japan by Dai Nippon Printing Co., Ltd., Tokyo, Japan.

ACKNOWLEDGEMENTS

For their special contributions, we wish to thank Jack Atlas; Timothy Burke, Hollywood Studio Museum; Esme Chandlee; Jo Ann Christy; Smae Spaulding Davis; Gwen Feldman, Samuel French, Inc.; Kyu Il and Mi Ja Hwang, Hollywood Photo Lab; James Ishihara, A & I Color Labs; Mark Jacobsen, Jacobsen Photographic Instruments; Preston J. Kaufmann, Showcase Publications; William P. Koffler; Katharine Loughney, The Library of Congress; Hugo Maisnik, Myer Show Print; Janet Meehan; George Morgan, Morgan Litho; Mary Rapoport; Walter Reimer, Continental Lithograph; Marcy Robin; Steve Shapiro; Richard Sinclair, Sinclair Printing; Nancy Spaulding, MGM; Kohei Tsumori, Dai Nippon Printing (America); Bruce Torrence, and David Wilde. Sincere appreciation to the staff of the Margaret Herrick Library at the Academy of Motion Picture Arts and Sciences and Academy Foundation, and to all the film studios for their generous help and cooperation.

FOREWORD

Like many another star-struck pre-teen in the mid-'20s, I can still recall my first movie love. He was, of course, Rudolph Valentino: the embodiment of mystery, love and romance. This great silent film idol accelerated the pulse rates of women ranging from tender years like mine to those of prissy, prudent dowagers who could scarcely admit to the frailties of their love-struck admiration. All of us were enslaved by his steamy, potent, magnetic screen presence. Those were the years of a budding era and of a budding industry that was destined to affect the manners, the morals, the fashions, the fads, indeed the lives of generations to come.

The images most of us had of those idols of the early days and, I believe, still have are the boldly colored, romanticized poses that arrested our attention as we strolled by our favorite entertainment center, our local movie theatre. It's the picture my mind retains of Valentino—*The Sheik*. Little did I suspect, or dare to think, that one day my own likeness would be emblazoned on similar movie posters and lobby cards.

My entry into the magical theatrical world was engineered by my father, Richard Bennett, a matinee idol of that time. At eighteen, still closer to childhood than adulthood, I was nevertheless the mother of my first daughter—and divorced. Father solved the dilemma of supporting my child by offering me a role in his current play, *Jarnegan*. It was a matter of mere months before fate took a part in my future in the person of Samuel Goldwyn. The West Coast moguls, confronted by the success of the new talkies and saddled with screen stars who had impossible speaking voices, had turned to the legitimate stage for a solution. Mr. Goldwyn (to the chagrin of my father who wished to take our play on a national tour) offered me a contract without requiring a screen test. Mother, a former actress who had become a literary agent, negotiated a release from my run-of-the-play contract, and I became Ronald Colman's leading lady in his first talking picture, *Bulldog Drummond*.

A first experience is always a most vivid one. It is nearly impossible for me to convey the feelings and emotions of those early days of my career. I had entered a dream world that would soon become a living reality. I was suddenly working with a celebrated, distinguished actor who was also one of Hollywood's idealized leading men. I found him handsome, suave and debonair but, above all, kind. Gently, he guided and instructed this stranger to a new medium in the subtleties and nuances of film acting, imparting a foundation of knowledge that I utilized throughout my motion picture career.

Over the years I was the beneficiary of similar kindnesses from other luminaries, each of whom shone with his own distinctive glow. There was not one who did not add some new facet to my growing compendium of experience: Spencer Tracy, Cary Grant, Bing Crosby, James Mason, Robert Montgomery, Gregory Peck, Robert Preston, Fredric March, George Arliss, John Barrymore, Edward G. Robinson, George Raft, Charles Boyer, Douglas Fairbanks Jr., Joel McCrea, Fred MacMurray, Warner Baxter and Humphrey Bogart.

As I thread my way through the following pages of reminiscences, I'm projected back into that time warp so popular with contemporary movie makers. In all honesty I find, reaffirmed, the delights of the past that seem so sorely lacking in our modern society.

Joan Bennett

—*Joan Bennett*

THE MICHAEL HAWKS COLLECTION

I've been a collector all my life. As a kid growing up in Oregon, I started with models—airplanes, ships and cars—and then moved on to stamps and coins. By the time I left school and was drafted into military service, my interests had changed and these boyhood collections were either sold or stored away.

If there is a single thread that ties together all the phases of collecting in my life, it's my fascination with actually holding something "old," a genuine article from a specific period of time. For me, there's wonderment in survival itself. But it's never enough: I also want to satisfy my need to know all about the history of that object.

I'd always been a movie fan, with a preference for the early films and silents. In my small home town there was little access to old movies, but occasionally they'd appear on late night television. Although I'd bought a few photographs from these early films by mail order through a New York store, it didn't occur to me to start a collection. It wasn't until I moved to Los Angeles in the late '60s and happened to find a bookstore on Hollywood Boulevard that specialized in film and theatrical memorabilia that I discovered lobby cards, a movie collectible that immediately appealed to me.

The first lobby card that ever caught my attention was for *Bonnie and Clyde*. It was propped up on a counter, the subject of discussion between a salesclerk and a customer. I eavesdropped for a while and then intruded on their conversation by asking a number of questions, beginning with "What is it?"

A lobby card is an 11 × 14 inch placard advertising a movie and displayed in the theatre lobby to entice moviegoers to the box office. Since the first flickering days of the two-reelers, lobby cards, posters and photographic stills have been issued by all the major movie studios to publicize their films.

However, my eyes had roamed past all the posters and photographs displayed in the store and had settled on a lobby card. I liked the format: the stiff paper was durable, and the cards were of a uniform size and therefore easy to store. From the beginning, movie stills seemed to me to be too accessible. Movie posters had to be rolled or framed and, because of their fragility, required special handling and, very often, restoration work. Besides, even in the late '60s, movie posters had begun to find a discriminating market and were beyond my reach financially. Lobby cards hadn't yet been "discovered" as collectibles and were just scarce enough to make the quest exciting rather than futile. All in all, lobby cards satisfied my desire as a collector. I appreciated the design elements and, in talking with the salesclerk that day, realized that if I could locate cards from the '20s and '30s, I would find really fine artwork. Finally, lobby cards were historically significant, representing every film made.

When the customer decided against buying the *Bonnie and Clyde* card, I dug into my pocket for the $3.95 asking price and started my collection.

Lobby cards and posters, for all their aesthetic merit and lavish production techniques, are advertising material and meant to be disposable. With each new film, the theatre owner acquires an assortment of promotional materials including lobby cards and various-sized posters, the latter ranging from one-sheets (27 × 41 inches); three-sheets (41 × 81 inches); six-sheets (82 × 81 inches) to the billboard-sized twenty-four sheets. As is today's television guide, they were tossed out to make room for advertising the new entertainment. These lobby cards, salvaged from cellars and attics, have survived for a variety of reasons.

About ten years ago I met an elderly man whose job it was to travel a circuit of Southern California theatres changing marquee lettering and lobby displays. He told me he'd passed the old Palace Theatre in Long Beach as it was being demolished and saw workmen tossing boxes onto a blazing trash heap. He managed to salvage the last three cartons before they burned and discovered they contained '30s lobby cards, most of which are now in my collection.

A large trove of even earlier lobby card treasure was discovered when an old house was torn down in a small Kansas town. These cards dated from 1916 to 1931 and had been stored in a theatre that went out of business. An enterprising homeowner salvaged the lobby cards to use as insulation and there they remained for fifty-five years. When I saw this collection, I was amazed at how well preserved it was. There was no water or sun damage; no mildew; no mice or insects had fed on it; and there were no holes or tears—all because the sturdy lobby card stock had been clamped between floorboards and walls keeping a family warm through fifty years of Kansas winters.

Most of my early lobby cards, particularly those for the silents, came from the attic of two elderly sisters in Minnesota. A mutual friend who knew of this collection told me that their father had been a theatre organist in a nickelodeon and that the sisters had found stacks of "old posters and stuff." If I was interested, he said, I'd better have a look soon before they did any more house cleaning. As children, they remembered their father bringing home "cardboard pictures" from the movie house for them to cut up and play with. Their mother, an avid fan of the two-reelers, saved lobby cards of her favorites, accumulating boxes of them in the attic. Hundreds of these fine examples had been carefully stored and then forgotten for nearly sixty years.

About twenty years ago when I first started collecting lobby cards, I came across a large cardboard box piled high with them in the dusty backroom of a rundown store in North Hollywood. The owner wanted a buck apiece, so I picked out the best and returned for more as I could afford them. In those days my budget was very limited, but it was also a time when "finds" were plentiful. As my collection grew, and with it my knowledge, I started to look for "sleepers"—cards that would be overlooked by anyone who was not knowledgeable. For example, Humphrey Bogart's third movie, *Body and Soul*, 1931: he wasn't even billed but his image is visible in the left corner of the card. Cards such as these are of infinitely greater value to me than *The Wizard of Oz* or *Gone With The Wind*. Those magnificent films were so popular that more of the cards were saved than those featuring lesser known films or actors and therefore are more readily available to collectors. Over the years I've come to realize that perhaps ten percent of a selection of newly discovered material untouched by any other collector will be of value to me artistically or historically.

I've always been drawn to the very earliest lobby cards, plus many from the '20s and '30s and several notable exceptions from the early '40s. Lobby cards after World War II lack the printing and design quality of their predecessors. Soon after I started collecting, I was fortunate in acquiring lobby cards from the Triangle Film Studio, founded in 1915, where Mack Sennett made pictures. The earliest of these cards is *The Hunt*, with Ford Sterling, made in December 1915. For many years it remained the oldest card in my collection and because I'd heard of no others pre-dating it, I assumed that Triangle Film had originated the lobby card. I'd come across posters (one-sheets, as they are properly called) advertising specific film titles rather than promoting the studio itself, from as early as 1909. Also from that period, I found a flyer distributed by a studio to theatre operators detailing the promotional materials available for display purposes. It made no mention of lobby cards, either by name or description.

Then a few years ago, a friend told me about some lobby cards he'd found that he thought might be of interest to me. As he described them, I thought he was joking—until I saw the cards and immediately wanted them for my collection. There were four different films represented, with three or four lobby cards for each title; all were made in 1913 by 101 Bison Feature, one of several companies making pictures under the Universal banner. The films were two-reelers, less than twenty minutes in length, but considered features until 1915 when longer films were made. These lobby cards, in the original vertical format, predated the earliest cards in my collection by at least two years. I was struck not only by the unusual format but also by the soft tones of the rotogravure process in these brown, purple and blue-tinted images. I already had many fine examples of the delicately colored cards that were issued for black and white films such as D. W. Griffith's 1919 silent feature *Broken Blossoms* starring Lillian Gish, which is included in this collection. These were now my "dinosaur" specimens, adding perspective to my understanding of the evolution of lobby cards.

Five basic methods of printing were used to produce posters and lobby cards: rotogravure, stone litho, offset lithography, letterpress and the photogelatin process. Origi-

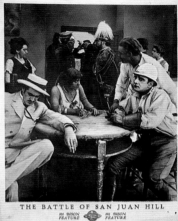

ABOVE LEFT: THE BATTLE OF SAN JUAN HILL—May 1913 • 101 Bison Feature—The man seated at left is Francis Ford, John Ford's brother.

ABOVE RIGHT: THE GUERILLA MENACE—June 1913 • 101 Bison Feature—Marshall Neilan and Wallace Reid. Neilan became a top director in the '20s.

LEFT: WOMAN AND WAR—June 1913 • 101 Bison Feature—Pauline Bush and Wallace Reid. Directed by Allan Dwan, who later did *Robin Hood* in 1922 with Douglas Fairbanks Sr. and *Sands of Iwo Jima* in 1949 with John Wayne.

nally, lobby card production began with a tinted black and white photograph that was often cut apart and pasted on plain backgrounds or assembled into a montage of other photographs or drawings. Hand-lettered titles and credits were added to complete the card. Wally Reimer (Continental Lithograph; Cleveland, Ohio) recalls that the wife of one of the printers would often take black and white photographs home and hand-color them to suit her own taste. "They'd give her six dollars to do eight of 'em," Reimer said. It's no wonder the colors of the stars' hair and complexions were often different from the film to the lobby card.

Most lobby cards and posters were printed on the East Coast or in the Mid-West, since the head offices of the major studios were in New York at that time. There were a few printers located in the West and one, Myer Show Print of Los Angeles, still prints posters for the Hollywood Studios.

All of these printing companies employed large art departments to churn out the massive quantity of advertising material needed to support the hundreds of films produced each year. George Morgan of Cleveland, Ohio, whose great-grandfather founded Morgan Litho in 1866, says that at one time the art department, numbering over 100 employees, produced the posters and lobby cards for all the major studios. Ninety presses rolled out the publicity material. Giant trucks departed daily to carry the art work from their 40,000 square-foot warehouse to National Screen Service's regional distribution centers. Morgan also recalls Howard Hughes sending an oil painting of the voluptuous Jane Russell in a low-cut blouse to Morgan Litho to make up the cards and posters for *The Outlaw* (1943). An armed guard brought the painting to Cleveland and accompanied it through each step of the printing process. Once the job was completed, the guard departed with the precious picture tucked under his arm to return it to Hughes in Hollywood.

Photogelatin was the printing method most widely used to produce lobby cards from the '20s to the '50s. A metal plate covered with a light-sensitive gelatin is exposed using a continuous-tone photographic negative. The gelatin's hardness depends on the amount of light passing through the negative; the darkest areas becoming the heaviest. When on the press, the heavy portions accept the most ink and are printed darkest. The lighter areas print lighter and give subtle gradations without using a screen of dots, as does lithography or letterpress. These delicate gradations were responsible for the beautiful flesh tones found in lobby cards of this era. However, there were two problems with the photogelatin process: special inks were required and it was necessary to maintain 80% humidity to enable the inks to adhere to the heavy card stock.

The highly individualistic artist/printers had their own formulas for producing colored inks. Hugo Maisnik (Myer Show Print) remembers one eccentric man who felt he was working in too-close proximity to his colleagues. He curtained off his booth for privacy while mixing his colors in order to keep his formula a secret.

The studios printed enormous quantities of lobby cards for each film, but most of them were discarded after the movie had played its run. On rare occasions, a quantity of these old cards are found preserved.

An East Coast collector recently showed me photographs of early lobby cards he said had been discovered a few years ago in an old building being renovated in Philadelphia.

In tearing down a wall, a room was discovered that had been a Universal exchange office until 1915 and then a storeroom for an astounding accumulation of posters and stills. The entire find was to be donated to a museum. I'm grateful that this rare and historically significant cache was not destroyed; but I'm saddened to think its final resting place may well be a museum warehouse where the cards will be "buried".

That's the voice of a collector you hear. Constant search and trading keeps existing cards in circulation, generates a healthy and lively appreciation of our heritage, and ensures that this art form will not be lost or forgotten.

The "marketplace" for collectors comprises conventions, stores and newsletters that specialize in movie memorabilia. Everyone has a special interest and if I can satisfy someone's need for '50s science fiction titles and thereby acquire a rare two-reeler silent card for myself, it's a good trade. I know a fellow collector who traded his living room sofa for a *King Kong* card. Money also changes hands. When I first started collecting, no card was valued at more than twenty-five dollars. Now, for an average card with a popular title and recognizable stars, one would expect to pay between one-and two-hundred dollars—and we've gone over the thousand dollar threshold on many titles. Eight years ago I bought a *Dracula* card for the bargain price of thirty-five dollars—its market value then was five-hundred dollars. Four years ago I sold it for three-thousand dollars and I know its value today is at least four-thousand dollars.

At the top of my current "shopping list" is *The Bride of Frankenstein* with Boris Karloff. There are also hundreds of other titles, many of them obscure, but they will complete my sets on particular stars or films. It's standard to have eight cards to a set.

Generally there's one title card, which usually has a superior graphic design and contains the primary credit information; the accompanying seven are scene cards. In the '50s, many studios dropped the title card and issued scene cards with little artwork. Disney was the holdout—they continued to do eight cards, including a title card, and maintained a high quality of design. In the '30s, Paramount dropped title cards almost completely, retaining the tradition for only a few select titles.

For a few movies, studios issued sets of sixteen cards and I have one complete set of these in my collection: the 1925 version of *Phantom of the Opera*. The sixteen-card sets that I've seen are all from Universal and include both 1926 and 1936 versions of *Showboat*, *The Hunchback of Notre Dame* (1923) and *All Quiet on the Western Front* (1930). The sets contain two title cards, plus fourteen accompanying scene cards with variations in borders and overall artwork.

In another break with tradition, Warners printed lobby cards on a coated linen paper from 1936 to early 1942. (On rare occasions—*Wings*, for example—I've come across Fox and Paramount titles printed on this durable stock.) Warners issued additional lobby cards for some of the same titles on the customary uncoated stock. I've heard two explanations for this anomaly: the less expensive cards were intended for either '40s re-releases or for second-or-third-run theatres.

Recently, while appraising a collection of lobby cards from the '20s, I discovered a rare set of 23 different scene cards in sepia tones (the title card missing) from a 1921 First National film, *Man, Woman, Marriage*. At the beginning of the sound era, this company, which produced the first *Tarzan of the Apes* film, merged with Warner Bros.

The very nature of the free-wheeling, ever-changing film industry makes research difficult. It's only in recent years that our film heritage has been explored and documented, and the accomplishments of those early craftsmen given value as art. In the meantime, records have been lost, names forgotten, studios and theatres destroyed. Much of the satisfaction I find in collecting is gleaned from piecing together information about a discovery and sharing it with other collectors.

After nearly twenty years of collecting, including several years working in a store specializing in memorabilia, I think I can readily spot another collector. Too often, however, I get a sinking sensation when someone approaches the counter carrying a lobby card or poster (often framed) and, fixing me with a conspiratorial eye, quietly asks "What'd'ya think it's worth?" Most of the time I have to disappoint him by looking at a chart, quoting a price around $5.95, and showing him a catalog that lists similar reproductions available in quantity. One persistent customer, finally convinced that his *Son of the Sheik* card was a copy, suggested that even so it might someday be valuable if he kept it long enough. I assured him it was valuable now—to him.

Copies abound—and I'm glad of it. The top dollar, of course, goes to the original prints of these lobby cards, along with the infinite pleasure a collector finds in simply holding a genuine vintage card. However, the design elements, artwork, historical significance and nostalgia for fine old films can be more widely enjoyed and appreciated because of the abundance of reproductions. Lobby cards—a dying art form—are now recognized as a valuable treasure from our past, meant to be shared.

By the way, if you happen to come across a *Bride of Frankenstein* card....

—*Michael Hawks*

LOBBY CARDS: THE CLASSIC FILMS

BROKEN BLOSSOMS

1 9 1 9 · United Artists

Filming entirely in a studio, Griffith effectively created the foggy, bleak atmosphere of London's Limehouse district. Barthelmess plays a chaste young Chinese in London who falls in love with Gish, daughter of a sadistic boxer (Crisp). The young man takes her in after she runs away, but the father finds her and beats her to death. Barthelmess, who has refrained from expressing his love for her, discovers the body, kills the father and then commits suicide. Gish, nearly thirty at the time, is entirely believable as the young girl. Crisp later directed *Don Q, Son of Zorro*. After *Intolerance*, Griffith's work had somewhat slipped in quality, but he regained his former glory with this film's commercial and artistic success. Usually seen today in black and white prints, this truly poetic film was tinted to emphasize emotion. Filming was completed in 18 days and nights without retakes or added scenes. The timing was so perfectly calculated in rehearsal and shooting that, when first run, the film was only 200 feet (less than three minutes) too long. It opened at a Broadway theatre at $3.00 a seat for top tickets.

STARRING: Lillian Gish, Richard Barthelmess, Donald Crisp
DIRECTOR: D. W. Griffith
STORY: Thomas Burke

OPPOSITE: *Richard Barthelmess, Lillian Gish*

D.W. GRIFFITH'S "BROKEN BLOSSOMS"

BEYOND THE ROCKS

1 9 2 2 · F a m o u s   P l a y e r s / P a r a m o u n t

Photoplay review, July 1922: "A little unreal and hectic as though the continuous presence of the stars was the desired
object." Elinor Glyn was the Jacquelyn Susann of her time, writing torrid, groundbreaking novels.
The story concerns a society girl (Swanson) who marries a rich old man to please her father. She's rescued from a
hiking acccident by an English Lord (Valentino). They fall in love, then part. Her husband con-
veniently dies, and the young lovers are reunited. This was Swanson's only film with Valentino (who had already done
The Sheik) because her contract stipulated that no other "star" could "co-star" with her. His name
does not appear on the lobby card. Swanson wore jewels worth more than one million dollars, and a wardrobe of
velvets, silks, sable and chinchilla. American censors demanded that kisses run no longer than ten
feet of film, so two versions were made, the European kiss filmed at greater length. Swanson commented: "Poor Rudy
could hardly get his nostrils flaring before the American version was over."

STARRING: Gloria Swanson, Rudolph Valentino
DIRECTOR: Sam Wood
PRODUCER: Jesse Lasky
WRITTEN BY: Elinor Glyn
ADAPTATION: Jack Cunningham

OPPOSITE: *Rudolph Valentino, Gloria Swanson*

DOUGLAS FAIRBANKS IN ROBIN HOOD

1922 · United Artists

When Robin Hood finally appears—halfway through the film—there are more than ten minutes of screen action uninterrupted by title cards. The enormous sets covered ten acres of studio backlot, and rivaled the cost and magnificence of D. W. Griffith's settings for *Intolerance*. A giant version of a child's slide, trampolines and handgrips attached to the high walls were some of the gadgets Fairbanks gleefully used to enhance his derring-do. His brother Robert played a practical joke, pretending that another film company was renting the sets for a day. An enraged Fairbanks was persuaded to watch a putative scene: a little fellow wearing a nightgown and cap appeared on the drawbridge carrying a kitten and an empty milk bottle. He yawned, set down the kitten and the milk bottle, ambled back into the castle and the drawbridge was raised. The figure was his friend Charlie Chaplin and Fairbanks loved the gag. The movie was a huge success and midnight screenings were necessary at Broadway's Lyric Theatre because the crowds refused to go away. Costume designer Mitchell Leisen became a famous director of '40s "women's pictures."

STARRING: Douglas Fairbanks Sr., Wallace Beery, Enid Bennett, Alan Hale
DIRECTOR: Allan Dwan
SCREENPLAY: Elton Thomas (Douglas Fairbanks Sr.)
DIRECTOR OF PHOTOGRAPHY: Arthur Edeson
COSTUMER: Mitchell Leisen
ART DIRECTOR: Wilfred Buckland

OPPOSITE: *Enid Bennett, Douglas Fairbanks Sr.*

"DOUGLAS FAIRBANKS IN ROBIN HOOD"

SHERLOCK HOLMES

1 9 2 2 · G o l d w y n

Sherlock Holmes was the first of William Powell's 95 films and one in which Hedda Hopper also made an appearance. This 64th Holmes movie (in which he clears a prince of a theft charge) was shot in London, Switzerland and the U. S. Barrymore, drunk and at odds with Parker throughout most of the European filming, was warned by the director that alcohol was killing him and agreed to abstain during the subsequent U. S. filming. Barrymore acheived Holmes' disguise as Moriarty simply by turning away from camera to muss his hair and contort his face. Two years earlier, in his famous portrayal of the dual roles in *Dr. Jekyll and Mr. Hyde* (1920), Barrymore had accomplished the startling transformations from one character to another without the aid of makeup. Renowned for his Great Profile, Barrymore was an inspired stage actor with a wonderful voice. The development of sound technology in film came too late to record him in his magnificent prime; however, even without the benefit of his voice, his fine acting talents and forceful screen presence are demonstrated in his silent films. Although his reckless, indulgent life-style presented difficulties during production, *Sherlock Holmes* earned good reviews.

STARRING: John Barrymore, Roland Young, Carol Dempster, William H. Powell
DIRECTOR: Albert Parker
PRODUCER: F. J. Godsal
SCENARIO: Marion Fairfax, Earle Browne
Based on the character by Arthur Conan Doyle and adapted from a William Gilette play.

OPPOSITE: *John Barrymore*

John Barrymore

in

SHERLOCK HOLMES

Directed by Albert Parker. Adapted from William Gillette's stage play founded on Sir Conan Doyle's stories

A Goldwyn Picture

SAFETY LAST

1 9 2 3 · P a t h é

After this film, Lloyd was known as the "King of Daredevil Comedy". A poor bumpkin who goes to the big city to make good becomes a department store clerk, but writes letters home to his girlfriend bragging about his important, responsible and lucrative job. To maintain the facade, he has to perform dangerous stunts for prize money. The story occurred to Lloyd when he saw Bill Strothers, a "human fly," scale a Los Angeles office building. Lloyd hired the steelworker as a stunt man but before filming began, Strothers broke his leg doing a three-story climb for recreation. Because scenes were shot on location in the Ville de Paris department store, filming started after closing hours and finished at two or three in the morning. The movie climb used straight photography, with camera placement emphasizing distance and perspective. Although there was always a platform or roof at some point below, Lloyd commented, "But who wants to fall three stories?" Lloyd got the girl both in the film and real life, marrying co-star Davis during the filming of his next picture, *Why Worry? Safety Last* was an enormous hit, breaking box office records, and Lloyd went on to become one of the wealthiest men in show business.

STARRING: Harold Lloyd, Mildred Davis, Noah Young
DIRECTOR: Fred Newmeyer and Sam Taylor
PRODUCER: Hal Roach
STORY BY: Harold Lloyd
SCREENPLAY: Hal Roach, Sam Taylor, Tim Whelan

OPPOSITE: *Harold Lloyd*

Pathécomedy
TRADE MARK

"Harold! Where are you?"

**HAROLD LLOYD
"SAFETY" LAST"**

THE GOLD RUSH

1 9 2 5 · U n i t e d   A r t i s t s

This great classic is Chaplin's most successful silent comedy and was equally well received when reissued with Chaplin's narration and a musical sound track in 1942. The film is about an Alaskan prospector, who becomes a reluctant partner with a crazed gold-hunter and loses his heart to a dance hall girl. The story idea came about during a weekend with Douglas Fairbanks Sr. when they looked at stereoptic slides of the Klondike. Tragic tales of the snowbound Donner Party perhaps inspired the whimisical Thanksgiving scene in which Chaplin cooks and eats his boots, savoring the laces as though they were spaghetti. Too many obstacles prohibited filming in Alaska, so Chaplin constructed his costly and exacting sets in the Rocky Mountains.

The production costs for the 14-month project are estimated at just under $1,000,000. Infatuated with 16-year-old Lita Grey, Chaplin signed her to play his leading lady and married her soon after filming started. Chaos resulted, with the girl's mother assuming control of everything in Chaplin's life except his film-making: there his artistic integrity allowed no compromise. He recast the role with Georgia Hale and remade all of Grey's scenes. Chaplin's two-million dollar profit from the film was exactly the settlement sought in Grey's divorce action. The universal appeal of *The Gold Rush*, which reflected American prosperity and Chaplin's own meteoric rise to riches, made it an immediate world-wide success.

Produced, Written, Directed and Starring Charlie Chaplin.
TECHNICAL DIRECTOR: Charles D. Hall
ASSOCIATE DIRECTOR: Charles Reisner
ASSISTANT DIRECTOR: Harry D'Arrast

OPPOSITE: *Charlie Chaplin*

CHARLIE CHAPLIN *in* "THE GOLD RUSH"

MADE IN U.S.A.

THE PHANTOM OF THE OPERA

1 9 2 5 · U n i v e r s a l

This film provided the huge box office success the industry needed in the year when free radio was introduced and movie attendence declined. With an incredible million-dollar budget, the highest since von Stroheim's *Foolish Wives*, Universal considered this their most important film of the year. The studio's concern was demonstrated in their considerable postproduction tampering, although the film ultimately released was very similar to Rupert Julian's original footage. Technicolor sequences were inserted for novelty value—the Red Death sequence was filmed in the 2-color Technicolor process and, in an otherwise black and white scene, the phantom's cloak is hand-tinted a brilliant red. As in many early films, prints in current circulation do not include the original tinting and coloring. Many of the prints now available are silent versions of the 1930 sound reissue, when the film was again edited, with operatic and dialogue scenes added. Films such as *The Raven* and *The Perils of Pauline* subsequently used the magnificent facsimile of the Paris Opera House with its main stage, balconies and five tiers reconstructed for the 1925 *Phantom*. Chaney endured tremendous discomfort and pain to acheive the splendid makeup effects: hooks in his nostrils, false teeth, celluloid disks in his mouth and clamps to pull down his lips. The film was a great achievement and earned huge profits.

STARRING: Lon Chaney Sr., Mary Philbin, Norman Kerry, Snitz Edwards, A. Gibson Gowland
DIRECTOR: Rupert Julian
SCENARIST: Elliott J. Clawson
From the novel by Gaston Leroux

OPPOSITE: *Lon Chaney Sr., Mary Philbin, Norman Kerry,*
A. Gibson Gowland

DON Q, SON OF ZORRO

1 9 2 5 · U n i t e d   A r t i s t s

This lobby card is one of the few with an artist's signature: George Holl. The original 1920 version of *Mark of Zorro* also starred Fairbanks as the well-bred aristocrat who masquerades as the romantic masked avenger.

After six weeks of constant work, Fairbanks became the master of the Australian stock whip. He amply demonstrated his skills by using the whip to put out a lighted candle, cut a contract in half, capture a wild bull and remove a cigarette from a villain's mouth. After seeing the film, children destroyed countless windows, vases and lamps with toy whips, emulating their hero. Actor/Director Donald Crisp's extensive dual career began with Griffith at Biograph in 1908. His acting career spanned 55 years and, for his role in *How Green Was My Valley*, he won the Academy Award for Best Supporting Actor in 1941.

STARRING: Douglas Fairbanks Sr., Mary Astor, Donald Crisp
DIRECTOR: Donald Crisp
SCREENPLAY: Jack Cunningham
From the novel "Don Q's Love Story" by K. and Hesketh Pritchard

OPPOSITE: *Douglas Fairbanks Sr.*

IT'S THE OLD ARMY GAME

1 9 2 6   ·   P a r a m o u n t   (F a m o u s   P l a y e r s / L a s k y)

The title refers to the shell game and comes from a post-Civil War expression used by drifters and con men: "It's the old army game—a boy can play as well as a man." The Army, naturally, objected to the use of this title. The plot concerns the misadventures of a drugstore owner who lets a con artist reverse the land rush by selling New York lots to Floridians. Critics complained that the material, based on the play by Joseph Patrick McEvoy with additional material from W. C. Fields' stage sketches, was hackneyed, "a shapeless collection of old skits." The movie barely broke even. W. C. Fields remade this picture at the same studio in 1934 as *It's a Gift* and it became one of his best known talking films. Former vaudeville actor Edward Sutherland, who was married to Louise Brooks, specialized in light comedy.

STARRING: W. C. Fields, Louise Brooks
DIRECTOR: Edward Sutherland
PRODUCER: Edward Sutherland
PRESENTED BY: Adolph Zukor and Jesse L. Lasky
SCREENPLAY: Tom J. Geraghty and J. Clarkson Miller

OPPOSITE: *Louise Brooks, W. C. Fields*

W.C. FIELDS AN EDWARD SUTHERLAND PRODUCTION

IN

A Paramount Picture

"IT'S THE OLD ARMY GAME"

WITH LOUISE BROOKS   FROM THE PLAY BY   JOSEPH P. McEVOY

THE SON OF THE SHEIK

1 9 2 6 · U n i t e d   A r t i s t s

Weary of reviews that cast doubts on his acting ability, Valentino chose to demonstrate his versatility by playing both father and son. He was deeply in debt and hoped that this film would salvage his finances and restore his public image as a virile leading man. (A widely read newspaper editorial had branded him "the pink powder puff.") The film was an enormous success and his popularity was so great that when he made a personal appearance at the premiere for this film, police had to contain a terrifying mob scene at the Strand theatre in Brooklyn. It was his last film; he died suddenly of a perforated ulcer August 23, 1926 at the age of 31. The desert scenes were filmed in Yuma, Arizona and many of the actors objected to the use of giant wind machines to create realistic sandstorms. Menzies, one of Hollywood's great art directors, later designed the sets for *Gone With The Wind*. Valentino's wardrobe, which cost a total of $11,260, included a sapphire-and-platinum ring ($4000), a gold-embroidered cloak ($500) and two jewel-encrusted belts ($600). Back in Hollywood during a break in filming, he walked by a movie set where Constance Talmadge was filming a snow scene for *The Duchess of Buffalo*. Valentino, in his elaborate Sheik costume jumped into the sleigh beside her, whipped up the horses and drove out of the studio into the sunny, traffic-clogged streets of Los Angeles.

STARRING: Rudolph Valentino, Vilma Banky, George Fawcett, Montagu Love
DIRECTOR: George Fitzmaurice
PRODUCER: John W. Considine Jr.
SCREENPLAY: Frances Marion, Fred de Gresac, derived from the novel by E. M. Hull
DIRECTOR OF PHOTOGRAPHY: George Barnes
ART DIRECTION: William Cameron Menzies

OPPOSITE: *Rudolph Valentino, Montagu Love*

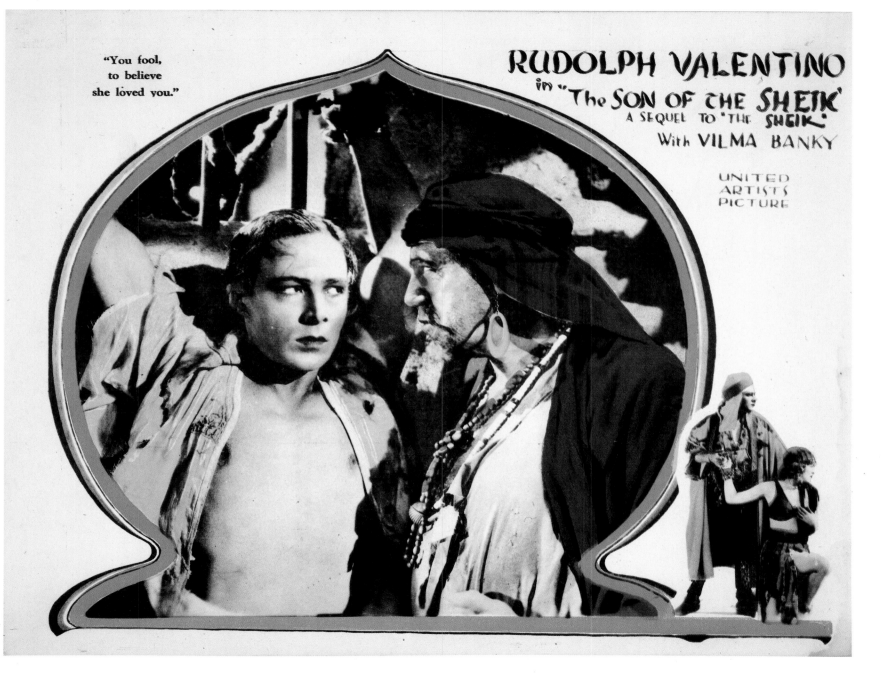

FLESH AND THE DEVIL

1 9 2 7 · M G M

This was Garbo's sixth film and her first screen appearance with matinee idol John Gilbert. An enormous hit, the film defied screen convention of the time by having the lovers play romantic scenes in a prone position and by using a remarkable number of close-ups. Their intense passion on camera inspired an off-screen romance that was highly publicized by the studio. Garbo on Gilbert: "He is so fine an artist that he lifts me along with him. It is not just a scene I am doing—I am living." Gilbert on Garbo: "What a woman!...Garbo has more sides to her personality than anyone I have ever met." Director Brown on the romantic duo: "They are in that blissful state of love that is so like a rosy cloud that they imagine themselves hidden behind it, as well as lost in it." After filming was completed, Gilbert proposed marriage and Garbo declined. Years later she dismissed the importance of the romance, saying: "I was lonely, and I couldn't speak English. And now I wonder what I ever saw in him."

STARRING: John Gilbert, Greta Garbo
DIRECTOR: Clarence Brown
SCREEN ADAPTATION: Benjamin F. Glazer, from the novel "The Undying Past" by Hermann Sudermann.
PHOTOGRAPHY: William Daniels

OPPOSITE: *Greta Garbo, John Gilbert*

JOHN
GILBERT
in
FLESH
AND THE
DEVIL
with
GRETA GARBO
LARS HANSON

Each embrace flamed with danger.

A Metro-Goldwyn-Mayer PICTURE

MADE IN U.S.A.

THE GENERAL

1 9 2 7 · U n i t e d   A r t i s t s

Keaton's personal favorite, this film is now regarded as his masterpiece and one of the great silent film comedies. The plot is based on a true story about a group of Union spies in the South who steal a locomotive and head north, sabotaging everything on their way. The train, named "The General," is recovered by its engineer, Johnnie Gray, who is the focus of Keaton's story. The state of Tennessee refused Keaton permission to use the actual locomotive on display at the Chattanooga station because they disliked the idea of a comedy about the Civil War. The filming (in Oregon) required 17 carloads of equipment from Hollywood and the services of 500 extras, the Oregon National Guard and 125 horses. In his quest for accuracy, Keaton used a real firebox in close-ups of the engineer's cab, which resulted in a forest fire. The scene in which the engine "Texas" collapses into a river was done in a single take at a cost of $42,000. The relic remaining in the river still provides a tourist attraction near Cottage Grove, Oregon. While most of the films at this time used as many as 300 title cards, *The General* featured fewer than 50 in its eight reels. Keaton's most ambitious film was a financial disaster and a critical failure when first released and resulted in his loss of creative freedom. Decades later it received the honors it deserved.

STARRING: Buster Keaton, Marion Mack
DIRECTORS: Buster Keaton and Clyde Bruckman
PRODUCER: Joseph M. Schenck
SCREENPLAY: Al Boasberg, Charles Smith
Story by Buster Keaton, derived from "The Great Locomotive Chase" by William A Pittenger.

OPPOSITE: *Buster Keaton, Marion Mack*

BUSTER KEATON in "The General"

UNITED ARTISTS PICTURE

WINGS

1 9 2 7 · P a r a m o u n t

Wings won the first Academy Award for Best Picture. Wellman (who appears briefly in the film as a soldier) and Saunders, both World War I ace pilots, were well acquainted with air combat and with the flyers themselves. No process photography was used—all aircraft scenes were shot in the sky. Dick Grace, one of Hollywood's best stunt pilots, provided two of the crashes. The movie was in production for a year at a cost of $2,000,000, not including the War Department's loan of equipment and uniforms in exchange for a picture that provided a good image of the Army Air Corp. Gary Cooper's role was small but memorable; the studio was flooded with fan mail for the "pilot who ate the chocolate bar and went to his death." Cooper was added to the picture as enticement for a recalcitrant Clara Bow, with whom he'd been having an on-again, off-again romance. Steamy accounts of her sexual escapades on location reveal amorous flings not only with Cooper but with several other actors, a writer and numerous pilots.

STARRING: Clara Bow, Charles "Buddy" Rogers, Richard Arlen, Jobyna Ralston, Gary Cooper
DIRECTOR: William A. Wellman
PRODUCER: Lucien Hubbard
SCREENPLAY: Hope Loring, Louise Lighton from the original story by John Monk Saunders

OPPOSITE: *"Buddy" Rogers, Clara Bow, Richard Arlen*

BULLDOG DRUMMOND

1 9 2 9 · U n i t e d   A r t i s t s

This was Ronald Colman's first talking picture. His cultured and resonant voice was a major factor in accomplishing
the transition to sound. Goldwyn's talent hunt for an ingenue with a good speaking voice led him
to eighteen-year-old stage actress Joan Bennett. Each scene was painstakingly rehearsed so that the actual filming was
rapid, with few retakes. The sets were constructed of cloth to baffle the sound and eliminate echoes;
however, action is stilted in places to accomodate hidden microphones. Lending prestige to the production was Sidney
Howard, the first well known playwright to do a screenplay. The film was critically acclaimed, a box
office success and earned Colman an Oscar nomination. Colman reprised the role in *Bulldog Drummond Strikes Back*
in 1934.

STARRING: Ronald Colman, Joan Bennett, Claud Allister
DIRECTOR: F. Richard Jones
PRODUCER: Sam Goldwyn
SCREENPLAY: Sidney Howard
Based on the play by H. C. McNeile ("Sapper") and Gerald du Maurier
ART DIRECTOR: William Cameron Menzies

OPPOSITE: *Ronald Colman, Joan Bennett*

RONALD COLMAN in "BULLDOG DRUMMOND"

UNITED ARTISTS PICTURE

TAMING OF THE SHREW

1 9 2 9 · U n i t e d   A r t i s t s

"All talking—All laughing." This was the first talking picture for Fairbanks, the second for Pickford and the only film they did together. Mary was struggling to change her "America's Sweetheart" image and Douglas demonstrated his discomfort by stretching his exercise period to noon, not bothering to learn his lines and refusing to do retakes. The film's reception did nothing to assure the stars of a future in the new medium. Critics panned the film, chastising Taylor for rewriting Shakespeare. The credit "Written by William Shakespeare with additional dialogue by Sam Taylor" isn't supported by the existing prints, and appears to have been no more than a joke at Taylor's expense. Production credits include the "Elton Corporation," one of Fairbanks' pseudonyms, so it's likely this was entirely a Fairbanks production. It was distributed by United Artists, the studio owned by Chaplin, Fairbanks and Pickford.

STARRING: Mary Pickford, Douglas Fairbanks Sr.
DIRECTOR: Sam Taylor
SCREEN ADAPTATION: Sam Taylor, based on the play by William Shakespeare
ART DIRECTION: William Cameron Menzies

OPPOSITE: *Mary Pickford, Douglas Fairbanks Sr.*

MARY PICKFORD & DOUGLAS FAIRBANKS in

ALL TALKING "TAMING OF THE SHREW" ALL LAUGHING

UNITED ARTISTS PICTURE

COUNTRY OF ORIGIN U.S.A.

THE VIRGINIAN

1 9 2 9 · P a r a m o u n t

This was Cooper's first all-talking film and an enormous hit. Shot on location near Sonora in the High Sierras, it was the third film version of the Owen Wister classic about the Virginia ranch foreman and his friend Steve who are friendly rivals for Molly Wood. When Steve is caught rustling and hanged, Molly blames the Virginian until the truth is revealed. The picture ends in a climactic shoot-out. Cecil B. De Mille's 1914 version was one of Hollywood's first features and starred Dustin Farnum. Other remakes starred Kenneth Harlan in 1923 and Joel McCrea in 1946. A weekly TV series beginning in 1962 starred James Drury. In the Cooper version, Richard Dix, Paramount's leading man at the time, had been set to star but demanded an excessive salary. When he left for RKO, Fleming persuaded Paramount to give Cooper the role. Randolph Scott, a Virginia native, coached Gary in his accent.

STARRING: Gary Cooper, Mary Brian, Walter Huston, Richard Arlen
DIRECTOR: Victor Fleming
PRODUCER: Louis Lighton
SCENARIST: Howard Estabrook, based on the novel by Owen Wister and the play by Kirk La Shelle

OPPOSITE: *Gary Cooper, Mary Brian, Walter Huston*

ALL QUIET ON THE WESTERN FRONT

1 9 3 0 · U n i v e r s a l

This classic film, a strong and powerful condemnation of war, is about the brutality and horrors confronting ordinary soldiers on both sides of the trenches in World War I. Milestone (who won his second Oscar with this film) directed with a fluidity and visual eloquence difficult to achieve with early talkies when actors were often required to hover motionless around a hidden microphone. In 1941 Lew Ayres declared himself a conscientious objector; while refusing to fight, he volunteered for noncombatant medical service and distinguished himself under fire.

DIRECTOR: Lewis Milestone
SCREENPLAY: Del Andrews, Maxwell Anderson, George Abbott
Based on the novel by Erich Maria Remarque
DIRECTOR OF PHOTOGRAPHY: Arthur Edeson

OPPOSITE: *Beginning fourth from left, Ben Alexander, Owen Davis Jr., Scott Kolk (also featured in the cameo), Lew Ayres, Louis Wolheim, Harold Goodwin, Slim Summerville, Richard Alexander*

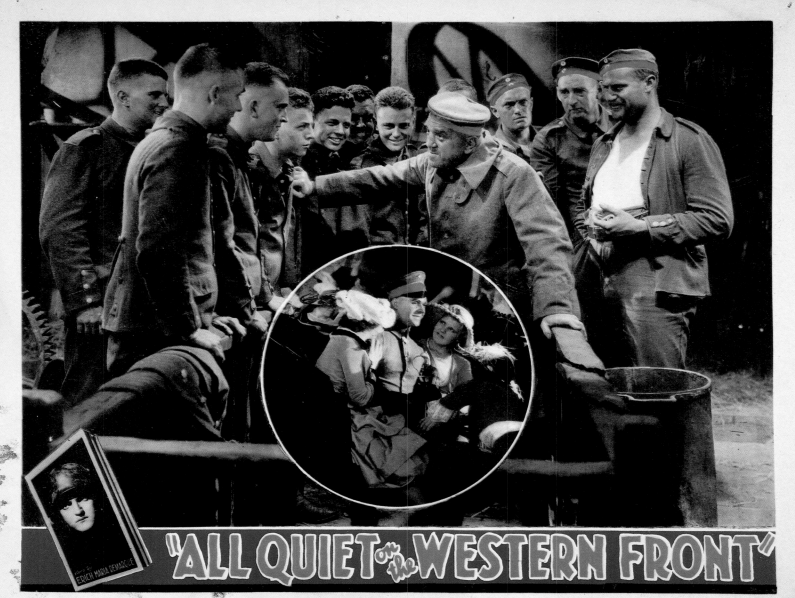

"ALL QUIET on the WESTERN FRONT"

ERICH MARIA REMARQUE

THE BIG TRAIL

1 9 3 0 · F o x

The film was a box office failure owing chiefly to its release in both 35 mm and 65 mm at a time when the country was in a severe depression and theatres, already trying to adapt to sound, could ill afford to convert to a large-screen format. This was Wayne's first starring role, and his easygoing, big-guy charm was already apparent. Poor box office receipts overshadowed this early acheivement, and it was eight years before his role as Ringo Kid in Ford's Western classic *Stagecoach* (1939) propelled him to stardom. Raoul Walsh had begun his film career by apprenticing himself to D. W. Griffith at Biograph as both actor and director; he appeared as John Wilkes Booth in the legendary *Birth of a Nation.*

STARRING: John Wayne, Margarite Churchill, El Brendel, Tully Marshall, Tyrone Power Sr.
DIRECTOR: Raoul Walsh
SCENARIO: Fred Serser
STORY: Hal G. Evarts
SCREENPLAY: Jack Peabody, Marie Boyle, Florence Postal

OPPOSITE: *Marguerite Churchill, Tully Marshall, John Wayne*

ANIMAL CRACKERS

1 9 3 0 • P a r a m o u n t

This was the second of five movies that the Marx Brothers filmed for Paramount. It was drubbed by the critics for being heavy, silly, static and incomprehensible. Nevertheless, it contains Groucho's most celebrated character (Captain Spaulding) in his greatest monolgue ("One morning I shot an elephant in my pajamas..."), and the theme song that much later introduced every episode of his TV quiz show "You Bet Your Life".

The film also features Harpo's famous silver-dropping routine. Legend has it that director Heerman, a silent film veteran, assigned an assistant director to each brother and also had four small cubicles constructed to contain them between takes. It didn't help; they were still tardy for set calls and prone to wander off during shooting. Despite everything, the film was a hit.

STARRING: The Marx Brothers (Goucho, Harpo, Chico and Zeppo), Margaret Dumont, Lillian Roth
DIRECTOR: Victor Heerman
SCREENPLAY: Morrie Ryskind, Bert Kalmar and Harry Ruby, based on the Musical Play
by George S. Kaufman, Morrie Ryskind, Bert Kalmar and Harry Ruby

OPPOSITE: *Far left, Margaret Irving, Groucho Marx*

THE MARX BROTHERS IN 'ANIMAL CRACKERS' WITH LILLIAN ROTH

A Paramount Picture

042 "COUNTRY OF ORIGIN U.S.A."

THIS LOBBY DISPLAY LEASED FROM PARAMOUNT PUBLIX CORPORATION

ANNA CHRISTIE

1 9 3 0 · M G M

"Garbo Talks!" A huge success, this was Garbo's 14th film, her first talkie. At first Garbo detested the O'Neill play because she felt it depicted Swedes as poor vagabonds and small-minded, bitter people. However, producer Thalberg was certain that she wouldn't walk out on the picture—noting that the Beverly Hills Bank where she kept her savings had gone under during the crash. The role of a Swedish girl seemed ideal for her introduction to talkies, but her English was so good that several scenes required retakes to make her foreign accent more pronounced. Marie Dressler on Garbo: "Garbo is lonely. She always has been and always will be. She lives in the core of a vast, aching loneliness. She is a great artist, but it is her supreme glory and supreme tragedy that art is to her the only reality." Garbo was so impressed with Dressler that the morning after she saw the film, she drove to Dressler's home and presented her with a large bouquet of chrysanthemums. George F. Marion reprised his role from the 1923 version starring Blanche Sweet.

STARRING: Greta Garbo, Marie Dressler, Charles Bickford, George F. Marion, Lee Phelps
DIRECTOR: Clarence Brown
ADAPTATION BY: Frances Marion, from the play by Eugene O'Neill
PHOTOGRAPHY: William Daniels

OPPOSITE: *George F. Marion, Greta Garbo*

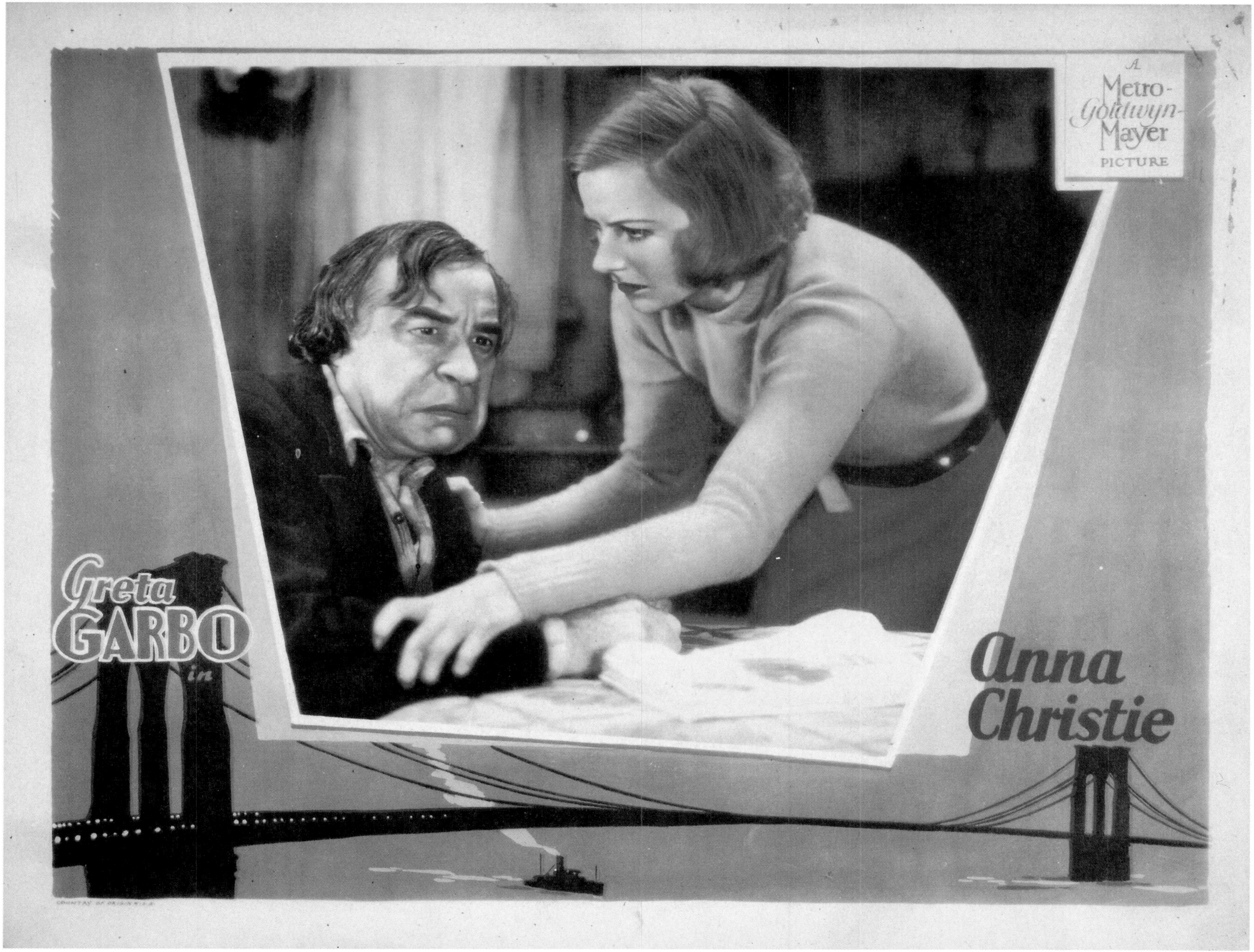
A Metro-Goldwyn-Mayer PICTURE
Greta GARBO in
Anna Christie

MOBY DICK

1 9 3 0 · W a r n e r   B r o s

This remake of *The Sea Beast* (a 1926 Warners film starring Barrymore) gave him a great dramatic role and ample
opportunity to simulate physical suffering, insanity and death throes—all of which he relished.

Joan Bennett replaced Barrymore's wife Dolores, who was pregnant. Noble Johnson, a black who often played Indians
and Eygptians, later appeared as the native chief in *King Kong* and Boris Karloff's servant in *The
Mummy*. The life-sized replica of the whale cost $12,000 and was manipulated by a two-man crew to do dives, turnups
and blows. Before its launching in San Pedro Harbor, the two operators were asked "Does it float?"

It didn't. The "whale" remains at the bottom of the harbor and the scenes were done in miniature.

STARRING: John Barrymore, Joan Bennett, and Noble Johnson as Queequeg.
DIRECTOR: Lloyd Bacon
SCREENPLAY AND DIALOGUE: L. Grubb Alexander
Based on the novel by Herman Melville

OPPOSITE: *Noble Johnson, John Barrymore*

MOROCCO

1 9 3 0 · P a r a m o u n t

Cooper plays Tom Brown, an American in the French Foreign Legion who gets involved with Dietrich, a cabaret singer. Von Sternberg, Dietrich's Svengali since he directed her in Germany in *Blue Angel*, lavished attention on her first American film, a property tailored for her. Arranging her camera setups left him little time for Cooper. Furthermore, von Sternberg, a Vienna-born American, had the irritating habit of assembling the entire company on the set to stand in silence while he directed Dietrich in German. It's said that on one occasion Cooper ignited von Sternberg's wrath by conspicuously yawning through one of these coaching sessions. When von Sternberg shouted at him in English, Cooper suggested that if the director spoke more English while directing, he might be able to stay awake. Despite these problems, Cooper liked Dietrich and they remained good friends. The movie was a big hit and earned Harry Miles the Oscar for Best Sound, with nominations for Dietrich, von Sternberg and Cinematographer Lee Garmes. The most famous scene is the final one: Dietrich slips off her high-heeled shoes and follows Cooper barefoot across the desert.

STARRING: Gary Cooper, Marlene Dietrich, Adolphe Menjou
DIRECTOR: Joseph von Sternberg
Scenarist Jules Furthman, based on the novel "Amy Jolly" by Benno Vigny

OPPOSITE: *Gary Cooper, Marlene Dietrich*

MOROCCO

WITH

GARY COOPER
MARLENE DIETRICH
ADOLPHE MENJOU
a
Paramount
Picture

"COUNTRY OF ORIGIN U.S.A." 3050

THIS LOBBY DISPLAY LEASED FROM PARAMOUNT PUBLIX CORPORATION

THE UNHOLY THREE

1 9 3 0 · M G M

This was Lon Chaney Sr.'s only talking film, the remake of a silent he had done in 1925. It was a huge success for Chaney who, disguised as a woman, plays the leader of a band of crooks. Sound was used to great advantage in a climactic moment on the witness stand. In his old-woman disguise, Chaney drops his voice to a normal masculine register and, utilizing his character's ventriloquist's skills, spares his innocent assistant's life by revealing the true story. Chaney, because of bad health, hadn't been able to do his first talkie in 1929 when many other MGM stars were making their debuts in the medium. Any doubts about the quality of his voice or his acting ability were laid to rest when Chaney (the son of deaf-mute parents) demonstrated his skill in this film: he not only played multiple roles, but provided voices for a parrot, a baby, an old woman and the ventriloquist's dummy. Through the publicity department, Chaney circulated a signed affidavit stating that he had personally done all the voices. A month after the film's release, Chaney died of throat cancer.

STARRING: Lon Chaney Sr. and Lila Lee
DIRECTOR: Jack Conway
SCREENPLAY: Elliott Nugent, J. C. Nugent, based on the story by Clarence Aaron Robbins

OPPOSITE: *Lila Lee, Lon Chaney Sr.*

DRACULA

1 9 3 1 · U n i v e r s a l

Billed as "the strangest love story ever told," the movie was released on Valentine's Day 1931. Universal had considered the property for several years but it was the success of the stage play in which Lugosi starred for three years, beginning in 1927, that convinced them. This film (based on the play rather than the Stoker novel) was a great success with critics and audiences alike. Browning was a famous director whose films include many starring Chaney Sr., among them the lost vampire movie *London After Midnight* and the original 1925 version of *The Unholy Three*. Despite the movie's popularity and Browning's successful career, the direction in this film is static and stagebound and the screenplay carelessly conceived and executed. Although Lugosi had made 15 previous American films and continued to work in pictures for another 25 years, his definitive interpretation of the Count is his most famous role: "I am...Dracula."

STARRING: Bela Lugosi, David Manners, Helen Chandler
DIRECTOR: Tod Browning
SCREENPLAY: Garrett Fort, based on the stage adaptation by John L. Balderston and Hamilton Deane

OPPOSITE: *Lower left corner, Helen Chandler; Bela Lugosi*

Carl Laemmle presents
DRACULA
The VAMPIRE THRILLER
A TOD BROWNING Production
with
BELA LUGOSI
DAVID MANNERS
HELEN CHANDLER
DWIGHT FRYE & Edward Van Sloan
from the famous novel & play by Bram Stoker
produced by Carl Laemmle Jr.
A UNIVERSAL Picture
Made in U.S.A.

POSSESSED

1 9 3 1 · M G M

Crawford plays a poor girl who goes to New York to make a better life for herself. She becomes involved with a rising
young politician and their secret marriage causes scandal. She provokes a quarrel to destroy the
marriage and save his career; predictably, they end up together. Shot in a record 27 days, this film was the third
teaming of Crawford and Gable and marked the beginning of their notorious romance. On-screen
and in real life, they were madly in love and, according to Crawford, "it was glorious and hopeless, like living over a
lighted powder keg." Both were married and their romance was doomed by the morals clause in
their contracts. A double divorce would have been disastrous for both their careers.

STARRING: Joan Crawford, Clark Gable
DIRECTOR: Clarence Brown
SCREEN ADAPTATION: Lenore Coffee
From the play "The Mirage" by Edgar Selwyn

OPPOSITE: *Clark Gable, Joan Crawford*

A Metro-Goldwyn-Mayer PICTURE

JOAN CRAWFORD in POSSESSED with CLARK GABLE

COUNTRY OF ORIGIN U.S.A.

THE PUBLIC ENEMY

1 9 3 1 · W a r n e r   B r o s.   &   V i t a p h o n e

The Production Code had been adopted March 31, 1930 and therefore the violence in this movie is suggested as much as illustrated. The famous scene in which Cagney shoves the grapefruit in his girlfriend's face was mentioned in every review and drew this comment from Mae Clarke: "I'm sorry I ever agreed to do the grapefruit bit. I never dreamed it would be shown in the movie. Bill Wellman thought of the idea suddenly. It wasn't even written in the script." Everyone claimed credit for the sequence, including the writers who said it was based on a true incident involving gangster Hymie Weiss and his girlfriend. Hymie allegedly used an omelette, which was deemed too messy for the film. In the shootout sequences, marksmen fired real bullets near the actors because the technology hadn't yet been developed to simulate live ammunition exploding. Wellman, who replaced Archie Mayo as director, continued his career-long exploration of strong, virile male relationships in this tough, funny, dramatic film about two street pals who rise from impoverished childhoods to become wealthy, unrepentent gangsters. After three days of filming, Wellman wanted Zanuck to switch the roles played by Cagney and Edward Woods, who was originally cast as the lead. It took some persuasion; Woods' wife was the daughter of powerful columnist Louella Parsons. Filmed in just over three weeks at a cost of $151,000, the movie grossed more than $1,000,000 and became one of Hollywood's first big-grossing low-budget pictures. Louise Brooks is billed as Bess, a bit role, but does not appear in the film.

STARRING: James Cagney, Jean Harlow, Mae Clarke, Joan Blondell, Edward Woods
DIRECTOR: William A. Wellman
PRODUCER: Darryl Zanuck
STORY: Kubec Glasmon, John Bright, based on the story "Beer and Blood" by John Bright
ADAPTATION: Harvey Thew

OPPOSITE: *James Cagney, Jean Harlow, Leslie Fenton,*
Dorothy Gee

THE PUBLIC ENEMY

a WARNER BROS. and VITAPHONE PRODUCTION

SUSAN LENOX (HER FALL AND RISE)

1 9 3 1 · M G M

A box office success, this turgid melodrama starred Garbo as a woman escaping from a father's brutality, acquiring a

"past," and then reforming her ways for the love of a man. That man was played by Clark Gable,

the studio's new sensation, who made ten films in 1931 and ultimately co-starred with every major actress on the

MGM lot.

STARRING: Greta Garbo, Clark Gable, Jean Hersholt, John Miljan, Alan Hale
DIRECTOR: Robert Z. Leonard
DIALOGUE: Zelda Sears, Edith Fitzgerald
ADAPTATION: Wanda Tuchock, based on the novel by David Graham Phillips

OPPOSITE: *Cecile Cunningham, Greta Garbo, Clark Gable*

FRANKENSTEIN

1 9 3 1 · U n i v e r s a l

This role brought fame to Karloff as the man-made monster created by the mad scientist Dr. Frankenstein (Colin Clive). Jack Pierce perfected the makeup which took four hours to apply and two to remove. To keep the monster's appearance a secret, Karloff was not permitted off the set, nor were visitors allowed on the set, during the day. Special boots gave him height, steel braces stiffened his arms and his wardrobe included a padded suit and a five-pound steel spine. Robert Florey, who did the original adaptation and hoped to direct, lost the assignment to James Whale. Karloff, who'd been acting since 1919, became an overnight star and Whale was established as a major director. *Frankenstein* made $53,000 in its first week; the initial American run alone made $1,000,000. It was shown at the first Venice Film Festival in 1932.

STARRING: Boris Karloff, Mae Clarke, John Boles, Colin Clive
DIRECTOR: James Whale
PRODUCER: Carl Laemmle Jr.
SCENARIO AND DIALOGUE: Garrett Fort and Francis Faragoh
ADAPTATION: John L. Balderston, from the play by Peggy Webling
Based on the novel by Mary Wollstonecraft Shelley

OPPOSITE: *Boris Karloff, Dwight Frye*

"FRANKENSTEIN"
THE MAN WHO MADE A MONSTER

AS YOU DESIRE ME

1 9 3 2 · M G M

Garbo plays Zara, a Budapest cafe entertainer suffering amnesia. Von Stroheim, a notorious perfectionist who always went over budget, was going through a bad period of unemployment, and Garbo insisted that he be given work. This was her first film with Melvyn Douglas with whom she would later do *Ninotchka*. Regarding Nobel Prize-winner Pirandello's incomprehensible storyline, Douglas said: "I never knew at any minute what I was supposed to be doing. It was beyond the understanding of any of us." On Garbo: "I have never played with a woman with such an ability to arouse the erotic impulse. The fact that an actress lets her partner take her in his arms or presses her lips against his does not make a love scene; you have also to see the emotion that drives her to do it, and it is this Garbo conjures forth at the right moment."

STARRING: Greta Garbo, Melvyn Douglas, Erich von Stroheim, Hedda Hopper
DIRECTOR: George Fitzmaurice
ADAPTATION AND DIALOGUE: Gene Markey, based on the play by Luigi Pirandello

OPPOSITE: *Greta Garbo, Erich von Stroheim*

THE BEAST OF THE CITY

1 9 3 2 · M G M

This tough gangster film in which every major player, including Harlow, dies in a climactic gun battle, is more characteristic of Warner Bros. films of the time; excepting this one and *The Secret Six* (also with Harlow), MGM did not make gangster films. The story is an adaptation of W. R. Burnett's western novel "Saint Johnson," also filmed in the same year by Universal as *Law and Order*. Walter Huston starred in both. The story about an honest police chief and his efforts to bring a racketeer to justice, despite the interference of his corrupt brother, earned Jean Harlow her first favorable New York Times review: she was called a "distinct asset." Harlow's comment: "Another picture like that and I'll be telling people that the color of my eyes is shotgun blue. Honest, I don't mind being a heat wave, but there was a crime wave before I came along. Or doesn't anyone remember?"

STARRING: Walter Huston, Jean Harlow, Wallace Ford, Jean Hersholt
DIRECTOR: Charles Brabin
SCREENPLAY: J. L. Mahin
Based on the story by W. R. Burnett

OPPOSITE: *Jean Harlow*

THE Beast OF THE City

A Cosmopolitan Production

A Metro-Goldwyn-Mayer PICTURE

COUNTRY OF ORIGIN U.S.A.

DR. JEKYLL AND MR. HYDE

1 9 3 2 · P a r a m o u n t

This is a very rare lobby card and an unusual one for a horror film: the monster's appearance was customarily kept as a surprise for the audience. Mamoulian, a stage director who was brought to Hollywood in 1929, was a great experimentalist. This film, his third, displays a masterful use of stunning camera effects to create suspense.

Among the innovative techniques he introduced: the use of voice-over to reveal a character's thoughts, dissolves with one scene directly related to the next, and the diagonally-spilt screen juxtaposing the simultaneous actions of one character with those of another character. March won an Oscar for Best Actor in the role Paramount originally intended for Karloff. John Barrymore had played the part in a 1920 version and Spencer Tracy starred in Victor Fleming's 1941 production.

STARRING: Fredric March, Miriam Hopkins, Rose Hobart, Holmes Herbert, Halliwell Hobbes
DIRECTOR: Rouben Mamoulian
ADAPTATION AND DIALOGUE: Samuel Hoffenstein and Percy Heath
Based on the story by Robert Louis Stevenson

OPPOSITE: *Holmes Herbert, Fredric March*

THE MUMMY

1 9 3 2 · U n i v e r s a l

Tutankhamen's tomb had been discovered in the previous decade and by 1930, all things Egyptian were the vogue.

King Tut motifs were reflected in everything from jewlery to popular music, and things ancient and
supernatural contributed to the plots of many stories. Karloff, playing the mummy revived centuries later, believes
Johann is the reincarnation of his ancient mate, Ankhsenamen, King Tut's wife. Karloff spent
eight hours a day with his face covered in clay and was wrapped in 150 yards of gauze.

STARRING: Boris Karloff, Zita Johann
DIRECTOR: Karl Freund
SCREENPLAY: Jules Furthman
Based on a story by Nina Wilcox Putnam and Richard Shayer

OPPOSITE: *Zita Johann, Boris Karloff*

KARLOFF *The Uncanny* IN *"The* **MUMMY"**

COUNTRY OF ORIGIN U. S. A.

ONE HOUR WITH YOU

1 9 3 2 · P a r a m o u n t

This remake of a 1924 Lubitsch picture, *The Marriage Circle*, was filmed simultaneously in French and English versions. Lubitsch agreed to direct, but George Cukor (who had co-directed a number of previous Paramount films) was asked to step in as interim director when production was delayed because Lubitsch was still involved in his antiwar film *The Man I Killed*. Cukor: "With the best intentions in the world, I couldn't direct an Ernst Lubitsch picture. Ernst Lubitsch is what they wanted and what they should have had." When Lubitsch finished the other film, he took over. It was agonizing for Cukor, who was compelled by his contract to remain on the set. Because Cukor remained throughout the filming—and because Lubitsch did not reshoot Cukor's work—Cukor protested when his name was removed from the credits. The film got good notices and was nominated for Best Picture, losing to *Grand Hotel*. Cukor left Paramount and, with producer David O. Selznick, made several memorable films at RKO and MGM, including *A Bill of Divorcement*, *Dinner at Eight* and *Little Women*. In 1938 Selznick fired Cukor as director of *Gone With The Wind* only ten days after production started.

STARRING: Jeanette MacDonald, Maurice Chevalier
DIRECTOR: Ernst Lubitsch, George Cukor
SCREENPLAY: Samson Raphaelson, based on the play "Only A Dream" by Lothar Schmidt

OPPOSITE: *Jeanette MacDonald, Maurice Chevalier,*
Charles Judels

MAURICE
CHEVALIER
IN
AN ERNST
LUBITSCH
PRODUCTION

ONE HOUR
WITH YOU

WITH
JEANETTE
MacDONALD

GENEVIEVE
TOBIN

A
Paramount
Picture

RASPUTIN AND THE EMPRESS

1 9 3 2 · M G M

This was the first time since childhood, when they'd staged "Camille" at home, that all three Barrymore's had acted together. The casting coup was Thalberg's idea. It took a million dollar salary to sign Ethel, who had an intense dislike of the cinema. She accepted the job only because of serious problems with the IRS—then deducted from her taxes the luxurious Beverly Hills estate she rented while filming. When John met her at the train station, he urgently requested that she make Thalberg hire cameraman Bill Daniels. "He takes all these sweetbreads away from under my eyes. Garbo won't make a picture without him." She got him, and also insisted that the Russian Boleslavsky take over as director. She rejected the first five scripts and then, hearing that MacArthur had arrived in town for a rest, badgered him into taking the writing assignment. When he at first refused, she threatened to wreck his house and began by throwing a lamp against the wall. Reviews were mixed for the $2,000,000 film. The studio lost nearly $1,000,000 more settling a libel suit with Princess Irina Yussoupov, who objected to a scene showing her being seduced by Rasputin.

STARRING: Lionel Barrymore, Ethel Barrymore and John Barrymore
DIRECTOR: Richard Boleslavsky
PRODUCER: Irving Thalberg
SCREENPLAY: Charles MacArthur

OPPOSITE: *Lionel, Ethel and John Barrymore*

6
JOHN
ETHEL
LIONEL
BARRYMORE
in
RASPUTIN
AND THE EMPRESS
DIRECTED BY
Richard Boleslavsky
RALPH
MORGAN
DIANA
WYNYARD
TAD
ALEXANDER
SCREEN PLAY BY CHARLES MACARTHUR
A Metro-Goldwyn-Mayer PICTURE
COUNTRY OF ORIGIN U.S.A.

THE MUSIC BOX

1 9 3 2 · M G M / H a l   R o a c h

This was Laurel and Hardy's only Oscar-winning film, receiving the award for Best Live-Action Short. It was shot in sequence and completed in a few days. The entire three-reeler is devoted to just one gag, the misadventures of two deliverymen and a piano. It's pure Laurel and Hardy: futility aggravated by a total lack of appreciation for their inept efforts. Just off-camera, Marvin Hatley plays the piano.

STARRING: Stan Laurel and Oliver Hardy
DIRECTOR: James Parrott
SCREENPLAY: H. M. Walker

OPPOSITE: *Billy Gilbert, Stan Laurel, Oliver Hardy*

STAN LAUREL · OLIVER HARDY
IN
THE MUSIC BOX

SHANGHAI EXPRESS

1 9 3 2 · P a r a m o u n t

Marlene Dietrich, as Shanghai Lily, offers herself to a rebel leader to save her lover's life in this spy story set in China on an express train. According to Jesse Lasky, von Sternberg's habit of directing while shouting through a megaphone cost him his voice during filming, so he set up a microphone. While staging an intimate scene between Marlene and Clive, he was almost breathing in their faces, yet still talking into the microphone. Von Sternberg had become very vain and relished acting out all the parts, including that of Anna May Wong, a rendering that was particularly hilarious. This was Dietrich's biggest hit to date and the audience delighted in her world-weary wit. The film is noted for Lee Garmes' stunning photography; it was his fourth and final film with Von Sternberg.

STARRING: Marlene Dietrich, Clive Brook, Anna Mae Wong, Warner Oland
DIRECTOR: Joseph von Sternberg
SCREENPLAY: Jules Furthman

OPPOSITE: *Marlene Dietrich, Clive Brook*

MARLENE
DIETRICH
IN
SHANGHAI
EXPRESS
WITH
CLIVE BROOK
ANNA MAY WONG
WARNER OLAND AND
EUGENE PALLETTE
Directed by
JOSEF von STERNBERG
a
Paramount
Picture

TODAY WE LIVE

1 9 3 3 · M G M

Despite the legendary talents involved, the picture was not a success. In this World War I melodrama, Joan Crawford is miscast as an aristocratic English girl (who did not appear in the original story). Crawford's American boarder (Cooper) and her girlhood sweetheart (Young) are together in the frontlines. When Cooper is reported dead, Crawford turns to Young. Cooper returns, becomes aware of his friends' romantic relationship, and volunteers for a death mission. Young contrives to go in his place. Filming was delayed a week because of Cooper's legitimate claim that his heavy work schedule had left him exhausted. He was also unhappy because the studio had refused to loan him out for Mary Pickford's final film, *Secrets*.

STARRING: Joan Crawford, Gary Cooper, Robert Young, Franchot Tone
DIRECTOR/PRODUCER: Howard Hawks
ADAPTATION: Edith Fitzgerald and Dwight Taylor
DIALOGUE: William Faulkner, from his story "Turnabout"

OPPOSITE: *Gary Cooper, Joan Crawford*

Joan
CRAWFORD
Gary COOPER
in
TODAY
WE LIVE

A Metro-Goldwyn-Mayer PICTURE

COUNTRY OF ORIGIN U.S.A

FLYING DOWN TO RIO

1 9 3 3 · R K O

This frothy musical romance is memorable for introducing Rogers and Astaire in their first screen appearance together. Rogers had 20 films to her credit but was not considered a major star. Astaire (who had scored great success on stage with his sister Adele as a dancing partner) had been given a minor role in *Dancing Lady* with Joan Crawford despite this verdict on his screen test: "Can't act. Slightly bald. Can dance a little." Astaire was so pessimistic about his movie debut, as well as the future of dance in film, that he avoided seeing a screening of *Flying Down To Rio*—and Rogers decided she didn't want to do any more musicals. The film was an enormous success. Astaire was signed to a seven year contract giving him creative control over his pictures, and his legs were insured for a million dollars. The rhumba-style carioca was introduced in a four-minute segment that took 100 hours to rehearse. Changes in film stock and lighting allowed designers to introduce the Big White Set, a staple of Astaire-Rogers films, that allowed cameramen to exploit maximum contrasts in black and white. In the original prints, the scene with Raul Roulien singing "Orchids in the Moonlight" to Dolores Del Rio was color-tinted. The finale, featuring girls festooning the wings of planes that fly over Rio Bay, was shot in a hangar; a few planes hung from the ceiling were activated by a wind machine. The film was shot in four weeks.

STARRING: Dolores Del Rio, Gene Raymond, Fred Astaire, Ginger Rogers
DIRECTOR: Thornton Freeland
PRODUCER: Louis Brock
SCREENPLAY: Cyril Hume, H. W. Haneman, Irwin Gelsey
MUSICAL DIRECTOR: Max Steiner
From the play by Anne Caldwell
Based on a story by Louis Brock

OPPOSITE: *Ginger Rogers, Fred Astaire*

KING KONG

1 9 3 3 · R K O

This movie rescued RKO from bankruptcy. Without its success the Astaire-Rogers musicals, *Little Women*, *Gunga Din* and *Citizen Kane*—among others—would not have been made by this studio. Many of the scenes filmed were cut, most of them showing Kong in an unsympathetic light (for example, chewing on natives and trampling them underfoot). The censors objected to a curious Kong undressing Fay Wray and also demanded that an English translation of the wholly invented language created for the natives be submitted for their approval. The famous climactic sequence of airplanes attacking King Kong as he climbs the Empire State Building with Fay Wray in his grasp is breathtaking. Production took over a year and the costly budget, resulting in the cancellation of other films, caused bitterness at the studio. Despite rumors about robots and men in monkey suits, all the Kong effects were stop-motion animation. The remnants of Cecil B. De Mille's Jerusalem set for the 1926 *King of Kings* was redressed to become the ruined city. Time Magazine named *King Kong* Movie of the Year in 1952, nearly twenty years after its first release, when it was re-issued and earned 2 1/2 times the gross that was then expected of a new film.

STARRING: Fay Wray, Robert Armstrong, Bruce Cabot, Noble Johnson
DIRECTOR: Merian C. Cooper and Ernest B. Schoedsack
EXECUTIVE PRODUCER: David O. Selznick
SCREENPLAY: James Creelman and Ruth Rose
STORY BY: Edgar Wallace and Merian C. Cooper
STOP-MOTION ANIMATION: Willis O'Brien
MUSIC: Max Steiner

OPPOSITE: *King Kong*

ALICE IN WONDERLAND

1 9 3 3 • P a r a m o u n t

The film drew primarily on Lewis Carroll's "Alice's Adventures in Wonderland," with some material from "Through the Looking-Glass." The movie, a 70th anniversary celebration of the publication of the Carroll classic, was stiff, stuffy and a dismal failure. Most of the actors appeared uncomfortable in their costumes and makeup, and audiences didn't like the idea of their favorite stars being obscured by masks. Gary Cooper, as the aging White Knight who continually falls off his horse, was one of the few fairly recognizable actors. Charlotte Henry played Alice, the role originally intended for Ida Lupino. W. C. Fields played Humpty Dumpty and Cary Grant was the Mock Turtle.

STARRING: Gary Cooper, Charlotte Henry, W. C. Fields, Cary Grant, Edward Everett Horton, Richard Arlen
DIRECTOR: Norman McLeod
PRODUCER: Louis D. Lighton
SCREENPLAY: Joseph L. Mankiewicz and William Cameron Menzies
Based on the story by Lewis Carroll
MASKS AND COSTUMES: Wally Westmore and Newt Jones

OPPOSITE: *Charlotte Henry, Gary Cooper*

Lewis Carroll's

"ALICE IN WONDERLAND"

WITH

CHARLOTTE HENRY

AS "ALICE"
AND

RICHARD ARLEN
ROSCO ATES
GARY COOPER
LEON ERROL
LOUISE FAZENDA
W. C. FIELDS
SKEETS GALLAGHER
CARY GRANT
RAYMOND HATTON
EDWARD EVERETT **HORTON**
ROSCOE KARNS
BABY LeROY
MAE MARSH
POLLY MORAN
JACK OAKIE
EDNA MAY OLIVER
MAY ROBSON
CHARLIE RUGGLES
ALISON SKIPWORTH
NED SPARKS
FORD STERLING

DIRECTED BY NORMAN McLEOD

a Paramount Picture

LITTLE WOMEN

1 9 3 3 · R K O

Sentimentality is avoided in this superb adaptation of the Louisa May Alcott story of a gritty family during the American Civil War. Oscars included Best Picture, Best Director and Best Screenplay Adaptation.

The simple house in Concord, Massachusetts, where Alcott had lived, was faithfully reproduced for the film. Costumes were made from plain, worn materials and the four girls traded them back and forth.

Joan Bennett had recently married and was pregnant during the filming. During this picture Katharine Hepburn began her tradition of bringing picnic lunches for the cast and crew. Hepburn, whom Cukor said was "born to play Jo," won the Cannes International 1934 Film Festival Award for Best Actress.

STARRING: Katharine Hepburn, Jean Parker, Joan Bennett, Frances Dee.
DIRECTOR: George Cukor
PRODUCER: David O. Selznick
ADAPTATION: Sarah Y. Mason and Victor Heerman
COSTUMES: Walter Plunkett

OPPOSITE: *Katharine Hepburn, Jean Parker, Joan Bennett, Frances Dee*

KATHARINE HEPBURN

LITTLE WOMEN

by LOUISA MAY ALCOTT

BOLERO

1 9 3 4 · P a r a m o u n t

This very popular picture starred Raft as a nightclub entertainer who never gets involved with his female dancing partners, including Lombard who loves him but finally gives up and chooses someone else. After returning home from the war with a weak heart, Raft does a "comeback" dance with her and suffers a fatal heart attack. The studio had originally planned to star Miriam Hopkins. Eager to return to the stage, and also disliking the role, she grudgingly agreed to do it only because it would be the final picture on her option. Carole wanted the role and urged Miriam to turn it down. Hopkins obligingly "fell ill" at the last minute and bowed out. Ironically, Lombard spent the final two weeks on *Bolero* commuting by air to locations on Catalina Island for *We're Not Dressing*, playing another role turned down by Hopkins.

STARRING: George Raft, Carole Lombard, Sally Rand, Ray Milland
DIRECTOR: Wesley Ruggles
SCREENPLAY: Horace Jackson
BASED ON A STORY BY: Carey Wilson and Kubic Glasmon
From an idea by Ruth Ridenour
"Bolero" by Maurice Ravel

OPPOSITE: *Carole Lombard, George Raft*

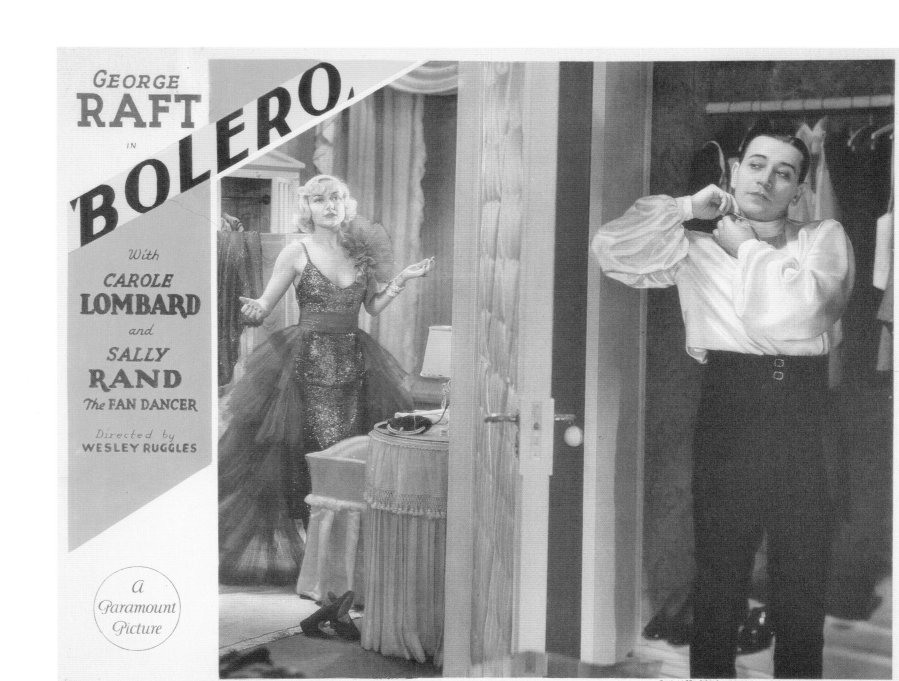

GEORGE
RAFT
IN
'BOLERO.

With
CAROLE
LOMBARD
and
SALLY
RAND
The FAN DANCER

Directed by
WESLEY RUGGLES

a
Paramount
Picture

CLEOPATRA

1 9 3 4 · P a r a m o u n t

Cecil B. De Mille had a reputation for bending the facts of history to suit his needs but he was passionate about
authenticity of artifacts: Cleopatra's hairpins were museum copies and the swords used in battle
sequences were real, not rubber. De Mille demanded that his actors fight to the death like real soldiers and Henry
Wilcoxon (as Mark Antony) recalls being challenged to a terrifying duel by the director himself,
who wanted to demonstrate realism. During a subsequent take, Wilcoxon's leg was cut to the bone and the end of a
little finger was chopped off. Colbert, who loathed snakes, refused to do the death scene with a real
one. To her horror De Mille arrived with an enormous tame boa constrictor draped around his neck and when she
protested hysterically, he whipped out a six-inch garden snake he'd hidden behind his back.
Colbert, much relieved, said, "Oh, the poor thing. It's scared to death." *Cleopatra* is lavish, opulent De Mille-style
entertainment with fine performances and Oscar-winning camerawork by Victor Milner. Box
office was good, but the reviews were terrible. Theda Bara did the first filmed version in 1917.

STARRING: Claudette Colbert, Warren William, Henry Wilcoxon
DIRECTOR/PRODUCER: Cecil B. DeMille
SCREENPLAY: Waldemar Young and Vincent Lawrence

OPPOSITE: *Warren William, Claudette Colbert, Leonard Mudie*

ADOLPH ZUKOR presents

CECIL B. DeMILLE'S "CLEOPATRA"

with

CLAUDETTE COLBERT

WARREN WILLIAM

HENRY WILCOXON

IAN KEITH

JOSEPH SCHILDKRAUT

C. AUBREY SMITH

GERTRUDE MICHAEL

A Paramount Picture

IT HAPPENED ONE NIGHT

1 9 3 4 • C o l u m b i a

This movie had everything against it. Columbia's Harry Cohn said, "Forget bus pictures. People don't want 'em." MGM's Mayer sent Gable to do "Cohn's lousy bus picture" as punishment for demanding a raise and asking not to do any more gigolo roles. Gable was furious at being sent to a second-rate studio and only Capra's smooth handling stopped him from walking out on his contract. In another fancy piece of manipulation, Capra persuaded Colbert, with whom he'd done a disastrous film in 1927, to delay her vacation and accept a $50,000 salary to shoot the film in four weeks. The budget was a tight $350,000, the hours were long and hard, and no one had any idea the movie would be a sensational success. It won Oscars for Best Picture, Best Screenplay, Best Director, Best Actor and Best Actress. It would be 35 years before another film—*Patton* in 1970—would win so many top awards. Gable got a new seven year contract and a generous salary increase following this success, besides the wrath of tee-shirt manufacturers for establishing the new he-man style of going bare-chested.

STARRING: Clark Gable, Claudette Colbert
DIRECTOR: Frank Capra
SCREENPLAY: Robert Riskin
Based on the story "Night Bus" by Samuel Hopkins Adams

OPPOSITE: *Clark Gable, Claudette Colbert*

NOW AND FOREVER

1 9 3 4 • P a r a m o u n t

Cooper plays a con man reformed by his charming daughter. Originally the film had a tragic ending with both Cooper and Lombard dying in a car crash, but Paramount felt it wasn't in keeping with the light-hearted story. In fact, it was because actress Dorothy Dell was killed in an auto crash that Lombard was brought in to play her role. This was Cooper's first film with Hathaway, who was to become his close friend and most frequent director. Lombard and Cooper got on well together and the film about a jewel thief going straight was a box office success. *Now and Forever* was one of nine films six-year-old Temple made in 1934.

STARRING: Gary Cooper, Carole Lombard, Shirley Temple
DIRECTOR: Henry Hathaway
PRODUCER: Louis D. Lighton
SCENARISTS: Vincent Lawrence, Sylvia Thalberg
Based on the original story "Honor Bright" by Jack Kirkland and Melville Baker

OPPOSITE: *Shirley Temple*

ADOLPH ZUKOR presents
NOW AND FOREVER
a Paramount Picture
with
GARY COOPER CAROLE LOMBARD SHIRLEY TEMPLE
Country of origin U. S. A. Copyright 1934 by Paramount Pictures Distributing Corp.
This lobby display leased from Paramount Pictures Distributing Corp. It must not be traded, sold, given away or sub-leased.

THE THIN MAN

1 9 3 4 · M G M

Van Dyke, who wore the traditional director's costume of riding breeches and boots, was known as "One Take Woody—rehearse it, do it, next scene"—and MGM loved him for it. William Powell joined MGM after Warner Bros. dropped his contract. Although Mayer was opposed to using Loy and thought Powell too old for the role, Van Dyke had seen their chemistry on the set of *Manhattan Melodrama* and insisted on casting them as blithe, carefree Nick and Nora Charles. Powell became the archetype of the jaunty, sharp-witted detective and he and Loy established themselves as a devoted couple in the modern sophisticated style. A delightful blend of mystery, romance and screwball comedy, this film launched a series of five *Thin Man* movies. Shot as a low-budget B picture in 16 days, the film grossed $2,000,000 in its first run and earned three Academy Award nominations. Powell won the Oscar for Best Actor. Photography was by James Wong Howe, the famous cameraman whose career spanned the mid-'20s to the early '70s.

STARRING: William Powell, Myrna Loy
DIRECTOR: W. S. Van Dyke
PRODUCER: Hunt Stromberg
SCREENPLAY: Albert Hackett, Frances Goodrich
From the novel by Dashiell Hammett

OPPOSITE: *William Powell, Myrna Loy, Henry Wadsworth*

WILLIAM POWELL and MYRNA LOY in "The Thin Man"

A Metro-Goldwyn-Mayer Picture   A Cosmopolitan Production

COUNTRY OF ORIGIN U.S.A.

20TH CENTURY

1 9 3 4 • C o l u m b i a

This zany comedy was John Barrymore's last starring role in a major picture and a turning point in Lombard's career. Paramount loaned her to Columbia, where she received five times her former salary. The story is about a shopgirl transformed into a star by a great Broadway producer. When she leaves him for a Hollywood career, he uses every trick in his extensive repertoire to lure her back to the stage. Among many who turned down the Lombard role because of Barrymore's drinking were Ina Claire, Tallulah Bankhead, Gloria Swanson, Ruth Chatterton, Constance Bennett, Ann Harding, Kay Francis and Joan Crawford. Being chosen as Barrymore's leading lady was an enormous career jump for Lombard. Both audiences and critics recognized her great talents as a comedienne, though she was so nervous and wooden in the beginning of filming that Howard Hawks threatened to fire her if she didn't stop "acting." Barrymore was the writers' inspiration for the role of the egomaniacal impressario Oscar Jaffe. The film got great reviews, but did only average business at the box office, perhaps because the "in joke" didn't appeal to the country at large. However, this film, along with *It Happened One Night*, brought prestige to Columbia and lifted the studio out of the ranks of B pictures.

STARRING: John Barrymore, Carole Lombard
DIRECTOR: Howard Hawks
SCREENPLAY: Ben Hecht and Charles MacArthur

OPPOSITE: *John Barrymore, Carole Lombard, Charles Lane*

JOHN BARRYMORE

COLUMBIA PICTURES

in "20th CENTURY" with CAROLE LOMBARD

ANNA KARENINA

1 9 3 5 · M G M

Beginning in 1935, MGM started using quotes from the film on their lobby cards. This picture was a remake of Garbo's 1927 film *Love*, also based on the Tolstoy classic. Anna Karenina, married to the bureauocrat Karenin (Rathbone), meets the dashing Count Vronsky (March). They fall in love and run away to Venice where she leaves him after a quarrel. When she sees him with another woman, she commits suicide by throwing herself in front of a train. Director Clarence Brown replaced George Cukor, who withdrew from the project prior to principal photography. Garbo broke her inviolable rule of never working past 5 p.m. by once working until 5:25, and the occasion was considered so newsworthy that the Associated Press sent out an item on it. The last scene by the railroad track is a masterpiece of illusion. Audiences, convinced they were seeing an incredible variety of emotions cross Garbo's face as she contemplates suicide, actually saw a single still frame with billows of smoke floating across it. David Selznick had urged Garbo to drop *Anna Karenina* and star in *Dark Victory*. Because of the disappointing box office on *Queen Christina*, he thought that another costume drama of approximately the same period would prove disastrous. Garbo elected to play Anna. Fredric March, too, had to be persuaded to do another costume movie.

STARRING: Greta Garbo, Fredric March, Basil Rathbone, Maureen O'Sullivan
DIRECTOR: Clarence Brown
PRODUCER: David O. Selznick
SCREENPLAY: Clemence Dane, Salka Viertel
ADAPTATION AND DIALOGUE: S. N. Behrman
Based on the novel by Count Leo Tolstoy
COLLABORATOR: Erich von Stroheim
PHOTOGRAPHY: William Daniels

OPPOSITE: *Greta Garbo, Fredric March*

Her voice trembled in an ecstacy of happiness and love. "I'm so happy," she murmured.

A Metro-Goldwyn-Mayer PICTURE

FREDRIC
Garbo · March
IN
Anna Karenina

"COUNTRY OF ORIGIN U.S.A."

CAPTAIN BLOOD

1 9 3 5 · W a r n e r   B r o s . / 1 s t   N a t i o n a l

Warner's acquired the rights to this project, among others, when they purchased Vitagraph which had done a 1923 version about Peter Blood, the physician, humanist and buccaneer. When Robert Donat, who'd won acclaim as the Count of Monte Cristo, dropped out of the role, it went to newcomer Flynn. The picture established his swashbuckling image, made him a star and signified a number of "firsts": the first of eight films with co-star de Havilland; the first of nine films with Curtiz; the first of his seven films scored by Korngold; and the first of many famous dueling sequences with Rathbone. Flynn was very nervous in the beginning, but his acting skills improved so dramatically that the first two weeks of filming were reshot. No full-scale ships were used and the town of Port Royal was mostly a miniature. Small ships, 18 feet long with 16 foot masts, were built in studio tanks, with the main deck re-created on the sound stage. The movie was a critical and box office success.

STARRING: Errol Flynn, Olivia de Havilland, Lionel Atwill, Basil Rathbone, Ross Alexander
DIRECTOR: Michael Curtiz
EXECUTIVE PRODUCER: Hal B. Wallis
ASSOCIATE PRODUCER: Harry Joe Brown, Gordon Hollingshead
SCREENPLAY: Casey Robinson
Based on the novel by Rafael Sabatini
SCORE: Erich Wolfgang Korngold

OPPOSITE: *Errol Flynn*

A Cosmopolitan Production

RELEASED·BY·FIRST·NATIONAL
PRODUCTIONS·CORPORATION
&THE·VITAPHONE·CORP·

CAPTAIN BLOOD

CHINA SEAS

1 9 3 5 · M G M

Gable did his own stunts in this film about a sea captain taking a gold shipment to Singapore and his problems with his sometimes-mistress, his new sweetheart, a typhoon, traitors and pirates. Nearly $1,000,000 was spent on the production, with a considerable portion expended on the typhoon that swamps the steamship. In Harlow's fourth film with Gable and her third and last with Beery, film critics praised her comedic talents and dynamic screen presence. Time Magazine ran a lengthy favorable review and featured Harlow (nicknamed "China Doll") on the cover—the first actress to be thus honored. Two years later, Harlow died of cerebral edema at age 26.

STARRING: Clark Gable, Jean Harlow, Wallace Beery, Lewis Stone, Rosalind Russell
DIRECTOR: Tay Garnett
ASSOCIATE PRODUCER: Albert Lewin
SCREENPLAY: Jules Furthman, James Kevan McGuiness
From the novel by Crosbie Garsten

OPPOSITE: *Clark Gable, Jean Harlow*

A TALE OF TWO CITIES

1 9 3 5 · M G M

This was Colman's favorite picture; the role of Sidney Carton was one he'd wanted to play since becoming an actor. Because of his intense interest in the project, Colman was at the studio throughout the filming, thereby breaking his professional habit of never appearing on the set unless he was working. Colman, who shaved his mustache for this role, received critical accolades for transcending his matinee-idol image. The picture took five months to make and ran over its million dollar budget because European locations were filmed to be used in conjuction with studio work. The film earned an Academy Award nomination for Best Picture.

STARRING: Ronald Colman, Elizabeth Allan, Basil Rathbone
DIRECTOR: Jack Conway
PRODUCER: David O. Selznick
SCREENPLAY: W. P. Lipscomb and S. N. Behrman
Based on the novel by Charles Dickens

OPPOSITE: *Elizabeth Allan, Ronald Colman*

"I gladly give my life for your happiness!" A love beyond love, keyed to the thrill of flaming revolution.

RONALD COLMAN IN CHARLES DICKENS' A TALE OF TWO CITIES

SAN FRANCISCO

1 9 3 6 · M G M

MacDonald wanted Gable for the role of the ruthless Barbary Coast club owner who hires her as a singer, and she waited without pay for him to be available. Although Gable didn't want to do the picture—he hated the idea of appearing with "some prima donna" to be "sung at"—he took the trouble to study "Frisco" slang for historical accuracy. MGM's research department got all the period details correct, and the San Francisco earthquake effects were the uncredited work of James Basive (who did the plague of locusts in *The Good Earth* and the effects in *Hurricane*). MGM reaped considerable publicity by hiring a number of old-time unemployed silents actors and inviting D. W. Griffith (who visited his former assistant Van Dyke on the set) to direct one of the mob scenes. The film got good reviews and was nominated for six Academy Awards, winning one for Douglas Shearer's Sound Recording.

STARRING: Clark Gable, Jeanette MacDonald, Spencer Tracy
DIRECTOR: W. S. Van Dyke
SCREENPLAY: Anita Loos
Based on a story by Oliver T. Marsh

OPPOSITE: *Clark Gable, Jeanette MacDonald*

Their love
survived death
and destruction in
the toughest town
on earth.

Clark **GABLE** Jeanette **MacDONALD** IN *San Francisco* with Spencer **TRACY**

A Metro-Goldwyn-Mayer PICTURE
COUNTRY OF ORIGIN U. S. A.

MR. DEEDS GOES TO TOWN

1 9 3 6 · C o l u m b i a

Longfellow Deeds, an innocent from the country, inherits a fortune and goes to the big city. Hard-boiled reporter Jean Arthur pretends to befriend him but sells his story behind his back. He's crushed when he discovers her betrayal and decides to give away his $20,000,000. When his attorney tries to have him committed, Arthur comes to his defense. Capra, who'd scored a huge hit for Columbia in 1934 with *It Happened One Night*, similarly brought out the best in Cooper and Arthur. Cooper, who got rave reviews, commented, "Just about the easiest acting I ever did...some roles that didn't turn out nearly as well were certainly harder." Jean Arthur, who'd just returned to Hollywood after some stage work, reaffirmed her magical screen presence. The picture won the New York Film Critics Best Picture Award and Frank Capra won the Academy Award for Best Director. Other Academy Award nominations included Best Picture, Best Actor, Best Screenplay and Best Sound.

STARRING: Gary Cooper, Jean Arthur
PRODUCER AND DIRECTOR: Frank Capra
SCREENPLAY: Robert Riskin
Based on Clarence Budington Kelland's "Opera Hat," a six-part serial in American Magazine.

OPPOSITE: *Gary Cooper, Jean Arthur*

Gary
COOPER
in
Mr. Deeds Goes to Town
with JEAN ARTHUR
a FRANK CAPRA PRODUCTION
COLUMBIA PICTURES
MADE IN U.S.A.

THE PETRIFIED FOREST

1 9 3 6 • W a r n e r   B r o s .

The play opened on Broadway January 7, 1935 and was a smash hit. Bogart played the role of Duke Mantee for 187 performances, but when Warner Bros. decided to do the film version, they wanted Edward G. Robinson to play the part. Leslie Howard, who'd starred in the play on Broadway, interceded on Bogart's behalf and refused to do the film version without him. Bogart reprised the role in a 1955 television production with Henry Fonda and Lauren Bacall. Bette Davis won fine reviews for her portrayal of Gabrielle, a waitress who wants to study art in France but is stuck in the Arizona desert at her father's truck-stop. Although the production was plagued with difficulties, not the least of which was the artificiality of the story line and characters, the film was a major triumph critically and commercially.

STARRING: Leslie Howard, Bette Davis, Humphrey Bogart
DIRECTOR: Archie Mayo
SCREENPLAY: Charles Kenyon, Delmer Daves
Based on the play by Robert Sherwood

OPPOSITE: *Leslie Howard, Genevieve Tobin, Paul Harvey, John Alexander, Humphrey Bogart, Adrian Morris*

LESLIE HOWARD
BETTE DAVIS

A WARNER BROS. PRODUCTIONS CORP PICTURE

THE
PETRIFIED
FOREST

MADE IN USA

DEAD END

1 9 3 7 · U n i t e d   A r t i s t s

Grim and gripping, this finely acted, well directed film about slum life in New York City introduced the Dead End Kids in the roles they originated in the Broadway hit of 1936. Bogart was loaned to Sam Goldwyn for this picture after a string of mediocre gangster films at Warners. One critic noted that he "turned in a first rate performance, streets ahead of his Warner Bros. films." The Dead End Kids—later billed as the Bowery Boys—were immediately signed by Warners for a string of gangster movies.

STARRING: Humphrey Bogart, Sylvia Sidney, Joel McCrea, Claire Trevor, the Dead End Kids
DIRECTOR: William Wyler
SCREENPLAY: Lillian Hellman
Based on the play by Sidney Kingsley

OPPOSITE: *Allen Jenkins, Leo Gorcey, Humphrey Bogart, Gabriel Dell, Bobby Jordan, Huntz Hall, Bernard Punsley, Billy Halop*

SAMUEL GOLDWYN presents

DEAD END

Starring **SYLVIA SIDNEY** *and* **JOEL McCREA**   Released thru
United Artists

CONQUEST

1 9 3 7 · M G M

This is a magnificent lobby card for a splendidly photographed costume drama that was a critical and commercial failure. The film cost $2,800,000 because of expensive sets, a twelve-month production schedule and a costly script that required a cast of hundreds. The photographic splendors included Cossack raids and an elaborate retreat from Moscow, but the result was blasted as shambling, episodic and lifeless. A total of some twenty screenwriters were consultants on the script. Boyer, who got good reviews and an Oscar nomination, commented, "I was fearful that to the French people no performance of Napoleon Bonaparte, not even a perfect one, would be satisfactory."

STARRING: Greta Garbo, Charles Boyer
DIRECTOR: Clarence Brown
PRODUCER: Bernard H. Hyman
SCREENPLAY: Samuel Hoffenstein, Salka Viertel, S. N. Behrman, Pani Walewska
Based on the novel by Waclaw Gasiorowski
Dramatization by Helm Jerome

OPPOSITE: *Charles Boyer, Greta Garbo*

Greta GARBO · Charles BOYER
in
Clarence Brown's
Production
of
Conquest
with
REGINALD OWEN · ALAN MARSHAL
HENRY STEPHENSON · LEIF ERIKSON
DAME MAY WHITTY · C. HENRY GORDON
Screen play by SAMUEL HOFFENSTEIN
SALKA VIERTEL and S.N. BEHRMAN
Directed by CLARENCE BROWN
Produced by Bernard H. Hyman
A Metro-Goldwyn-Mayer PICTURE
COUNTRY OF ORIGIN U. S. A.

THE PRINCE AND THE PAUPER

1 9 3 7 • W a r n e r   B r o s . / 1 s t   N a t i o n a l

A prince and a poor boy switch clothing and the prince, mistaken for the pauper, is driven from the palace. He is befriended by a soldier of fortune (Flynn) who believes him to be mad. The prince slips back into the palace and proves his identity by revealing the hiding place of the Great Seal. In the denouement, he is crowned king. This generated public interest because of the imminent real-life coronation of George VI, following Edward VIII's abdication. Flynn, who doesn't appear until halfway through this story, became fast friends with Hale during the filming and subsequently they appeared together in twelve pictures.

STARRING: Errol Flynn, Claude Rains, Henry Stephenson, Billy and Bobby Mauch, Alan Hale
DIRECTOR: William Keighley
EXECUTIVE PRODUCER: Hal B. Wallis
ASSOCIATE PRODUCER: Robert Lord
SCREENPLAY: Laird Doyle
DRAMATIC VERSION: Catherine Chisolm
Based on the novel by Mark Twain
SCORE: Erich Wolfgang Korngold

OPPOSITE: *Errol Flynn, Bobby Mauch*

the PRINCE
and the
PAUPER
By
MARK TWAIN
ERROL FLYNN
CLAUDE RAINS · HENRY STEPHENSON
and the MAUCH TWINS BILLY & BOBBY
ERIC PORTMAN
Directed by WILLIAM KEIGHLEY
A FIRST NATIONAL PICTURE
Presented by Warner Bros.
"Country of origin U.S.A. Copyright
Vitagraph, Inc. All rights reserved"

THE ADVENTURES OF ROBIN HOOD

1938 · Warner Bros./1st National

James Cagney was Warner's original choice for Robin Hood, but he walked out on the studio in a contract dispute. The script was then tailored for Flynn because of his recent success in *Captain Blood*. The initial budget was set at $1,600,000—the highest at that time for a Warner picture—and the cost eventually topped $2,000,000. After filming the Sherwood Forest sequences, director Keighley was replaced by Curtiz because Jack Warner, Wallis and Blanke felt Keighley's approach lacked dramatic impact. Curtiz directed all of the interior-action sequences, including "Robin Hood fights his way out of the castle," which took three weeks to film. Warner phoned the set daily to ask "Hasn't he got out yet?" Flynn, a born athlete, did most of his own duelling and stunts, although Rathbone was the master at fencing. The then-new 3-color Technicolor process (which became obsolete in the mid-'50s) was used to great effect. The film was a critical and popular success. Oscars: Korngold for Original Score, Ralph Dawson for Film Editing, Carl Jules Weyl for Interior Decoration.

STARRING: Errol Flynn, Olivia de Havilland, Basil Rathbone, Claude Rains, Alan Hale
DIRECTORS: Michael Curtiz and William Keighley
EXECUTIVE PRODUCER: Hal B. Wallis
ASSOCIATE PRODUCER: Henry Blanke
ORIGINAL SCREENPLAY: Norman Reilly Raine, Seton I. Miller
MUSIC: Erich Wolfgang Korngold

OPPOSITE: *Basil Rathbone, Errol Flynn*

THE GIRL OF THE GOLDEN WEST

1 9 3 8 · M G M

The story of an innocent young girl heading west who is romanced by a bandit leader is based on Puccini's 1905 opera. Enrico Caruso starred in the 1910 stage version, sung in Italian, that featured a horde of cowboys singing "doo-da, doo-da." De Mille had filmed an adaptation in 1914 with Mabel Van Buren. Warner released a 1923 version with Sylvia Breamer, then remade it into a talkie with Ann Harding in 1930. In the 1938 version the heroine is named Mary—rather than Minnie—to avoid any connection with either the mouse or the moocher. The film was panned, with critics complaining about its length and the dated plot.

STARRING: Jeanette MacDonald, Nelson Eddy, Walter Pidgeon
DIRECTOR: Robert Z. Leonard
PRODUCER: William Anthony McGuire
Based on the play by David Belasco
SCREENPLAY: Isabel Dawn and Boyce DeGaw
SCORE: Gus Kahn, Sigmund Romberg

OPPOSITE: *Nelson Eddy, Jeanette MacDonald*

Jeanette MacDONALD · Nelson EDDY
in "THE GIRL OF THE GOLDEN WEST"

A Metro-Goldwyn-Mayer PICTURE

"Your eyes sparkle like the blue Pacific!"

HOLIDAY

1 9 3 8 · C o l u m b i a

This frothy, delightful film (as well as *The Philadelphia Story*) was adapted from a play by Philip Barry. A young, free-spirited man falls in love with a rich girl. Since he's more interested in his personal pursuits than in getting a respectable job, he's considered a fortune hunter. The rich girl rejects him, but he finds his match and his mate in her unconventional, irrepressible sister. The 1930 RKO-Pathé version starred Ann Harding and Mary Astor as the sisters, with Edward Everett Horton playing their brother, Nick Potter, in the role he reprised eight years later.

STARRING: Katharine Hepburn, Cary Grant, Doris Nolan, Edward Everett Horton, Lew Ayres
DIRECTOR: George Cukor
ASSOCIATE PRODUCER: Everett Riskin
SCREENPLAY: Donald Ogden Stewart and Sidney Buchman
Original Play by Philip Barry

OPPOSITE: *Cary Grant, Katharine Hepburn*

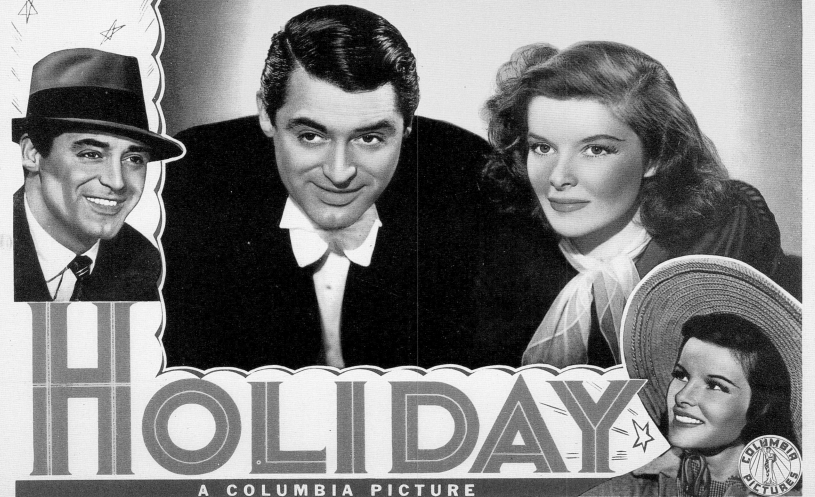

JEZEBEL

1 9 3 8 · W a r n e r   B r o s .

This film won Davis her second Academy Award for Best Actress. She stars as Julie, the spoiled belle of New Orleans; Pres (Fonda) and Buck (Brent), are her two rival suitors. As a dramatic gesture, she wears a scarlet gown to a Mardi Gras ball, where women traditionally wear white gowns. The town is scandalized, and Pres breaks the engagement. He leaves town but later returns with a northern wife. When he contracts Yellow Fever, Davis volunteers to replace his wife in nursing him back to health. The ball scene was shot without a word of dialogue. The infamous red gown was actually a deep-rust-colored satin, which appeared red—even in black and white. Davis wanted the film shot in color, but Warner considered that an unnecessary expense. Wyler, a perfectionist, shot 45 takes of Davis' entrance when she lifts her skirt with a riding crop. When he ran a month over the shooting schedule, Warner threatened to fire him. Davis, who had nursed a longstanding grudge against Wyler, nevertheless defended him. Henry Fonda's scenes had to be completed early so he could return East for daughter Jane's birth. Therefore, Davis had to shoot many of her close-ups without her leading man. The picture, adapted from a Broadway play, won praise from the critics and was a huge popular success.

STARRING: Bette Davis, Henry Fonda, George Brent, Fay Bainter, Donald Crisp
DIRECTOR: William Wyler
SCREENPLAY: John Huston, Clements Ripley, Abem Finke
Based on the play by Owen Davis
COSTUME DESIGN: Orry-Kelly

OPPOSITE: *Henry Fonda, Bette Davis*

JEZEBEL
A WARNER BROS. PICTURE

TEST PILOT

1 9 3 8 · M G M

Frank Wead had been an Air Corps pilot; after a severe accident which crippled him for life, he became a writer, primarily of stories about flight. John Wayne's *The Wings of Eagles* is based on Wead's life story. The Army Air Corps provided four different airfield locations and the use of B-17 bombers, the latest military aircraft, to exploit their publicity value. Gable was fascinated with the B-17 and persuaded a pilot to let him fly one, with the pilot giving instructions with the dual controls. A blend of romantic comedy and melodrama, the film was both a popular and critical success.

STARRING: Clark Gable, Myrna Loy, Spencer Tracy, Lionel Barrymore
DIRECTOR: Victor Fleming
PRODUCER: Louis B. Lighton
SCREENPLAY: Vincent Lawrence, Waldemar Young
Based on a story by Frank Wead

OPPOSITE: *Myrna Loy, Spencer Tracy, Clark Gable*

CLARK
GABLE
MYRNA
LOY
SPENCER
TRACY

WITH *Lionel* BARRYMORE

Screen play by VINCENT LAWRENCE   WALDEMAR YOUNG
Original Story by FRANK WEAD

Directed by VICTOR FLEMING
Produced by LOUIS D. LIGHTON

A
Metro-
Goldwyn-
Mayer
PICTURE

TEST-PILOT

VICTOR
FLEMING'S *production*

COUNTRY OF ORIGIN U. S. A.

ANGELS WITH DIRTY FACES

1 9 3 8 • W a r n e r   B r o s .

In the late '30s, gangster movies began to include a moral lesson to balance the violence. In this case, the gangster

destroys his image to prevent the local kids from following his example. Live ammunition was used

in the action pictures of the '30s and Cagney just missed being struck by a bullet. "Stupid," he said. "They were

dangerous, and I went on doing it for a long time with the wild bullets flying in all directions." In

this well cast, finely directed melodrama, Cagney got his first Oscar nomination and won the New York Film Critics'

prize.

STARRING: James Cagney, Humphrey Bogart, Ann Sheridan, George Bancroft, Pat O'Brien, the Dead End Kids
DIRECTOR: Michael Curtiz
PRODUCER: Sam Bischoff
SCREENPLAY: John Wexley and Warren Duff. Based on an original story by Rowland Brown.

OPPOSITE: *James Cagney, George Bancroft, Humphrey Bogart*

Angels with Dirty Faces

JAMES CAGNEY & PAT O'BRIEN

THE ADVENTURES OF SHERLOCK HOLMES

1 9 3 9 · 2 0 t h   C e n t u r y - F o x

Rathbone as the cunning sleuth Holmes and Bruce as the bumbling Watson, are a matchless pair. This film about
arch-villain Moriarty's plan to steal the Star of India from the Tower of London was made the same
year as the highly successful *Hound of the Baskervilles*. The two films—with their fine sets, splendid costumes and
faithful rendering of the Doyle stories—are considered the best of the series. In a memorable scene,
Rathbone's disguised as a music-hall entertainer and performs a song-and-dance routine. After 20th Century-Fox
decided this would be their last Sherlock Holmes film, Universal stepped in to do twelve more, with
both Rathbone and Bruce reprising their roles.

STARRING: Basil Rathbone, Ida Lupino, Nigel Bruce
DIRECTOR: Alfred L. Werker
EXECUTIVE PRODUCER: Darryl F. Zanuck
ASSOCIATE PRODUCER: Gene Markey
SCREENPLAY: Edwin Blum and William Drake, based on the play "Sherlock Holmes" by William Gillette
Adapted from the stories by Arthur Conan Doyle.

OPPOSITE: *Basil Rathbone, Ida Lupino, Nigel Bruce*

GUNGA DIN

1 9 3 9 · R K O

Hecht and MacArthur dreamed up this version of Kipling's tale about a water boy who wants to be a British soldier. This splendid action-adventure story is enhanced by the magnetic energy of Grant, Fairbanks and McLaglen. Grant played Archibald Cutter (a twist on his real name, Archibald Leach). RKO's biggest budgeted film to date, it rewarded the studio with huge box office returns, grossing $3.8 million. Contemporary reviews were mixed. Today, though sometimes berated as outdated and racist, the picture is generally regarded as a classic.

STARRING: Douglas Fairbanks, Jr., Cary Grant, Victor McLaglen, Sam Jaffe, Joan Fontaine
DIRECTOR: George Stevens
PRODUCER: Pandro S. Berman
STORY BY: Ben Hecht and Charles MacArthur
SCREENPLAY: Joel Sayre and Fred Guiol
Derived from the poem by Rudyard Kipling

OPPOSITE: *Douglas Fairbanks Jr., Cary Grant*

GUNGA DIN

THE HUNCHBACK OF NOTRE DAME

1 9 3 9 · R K O

On the day the bell ringing scene was to be filmed, England and France declared war on the Third Reich. Laughton went on ringing the bells long after the scene was over and when finally he stopped, completely exhausted, no one watching moved or spoke. Later in his dressing room, Laughton explained to director Dieterle, "I couldn't think of Esmerelda in that scene at all. I could only think of the poor people out there, going to fight that bloody, bloody war! To arouse the world, to stop that terrible butchery. Awake! Awake! That's what I felt when I was ringing that bell." Maureen O'Hara, Laughton's protégé, was escorted from London by her mother and Laughton to play Esmerelda in her first American film. No stills were released of Laughton in his makeup, which took three hours to apply and thirty minutes to remove. His two-pound hump was made of papier-mâché, and wires helped distort his posture. The replica of Notre Dame and the surrounding streets was constructed in the San Fernando Valley. Universal made a version of this story with Lon Chaney in 1923, but the RKO picture is considered the greatest of all adaptations and was a great success.

STARRING: Charles Laughton, Maureen O'Hara, Cedric Hardwicke, Thomas Mitchell, Edmond O'Brien
DIRECTOR: William Dieterle
PRODUCER: Pandro S. Berman
SCREENPLAY: Sonya Levien
From the novel by Victor Hugo
Makeup: Perc Westmore

OPPOSITE: *Charles Laughton, Maureen O'Hara*

MR. SMITH GOES TO WASHINGTON

1 9 3 9 · C o l u m b i a

An honest man does not realize that he has been sent to the Senate by corrupt politicians, and fights for his honor upon learning the truth. This role earned Stewart the first of his five Oscar nominations. When the award went to Robert Donat for *Goodbye Mr. Chips*, newspapers devoted more space to the loser than the winner, illustrated by a headline screaming "Jimmy was gypped!" The following year he won an Academy Award for *Philadelphia Story*; many feel that it was a consolation prize. *Mr. Smith* received excellent reviews, and won the New York Critics Award for Best Picture as well as an Oscar for Foster's Best Original Story.

STARRING: Jean Arthur, James Stewart
DIRECTOR: Frank Capra
SCREENPLAY: Sidney Buchman, based on a story by Lewis R. Foster

OPPOSITE: *James Stewart, Jean Arthur*

FRANK CAPRA'S

MR. SMITH GOES TO WASHINGTON

co-starring **JEAN ARTHUR** and **JAMES STEWART**

A COLUMBIA PICTURE

PRINTED IN U.S.A.

THE ROARING TWENTIES

1 9 3 9 • W a r n e r   B r o s .

This film about bootleggers, made barely six years after repeal of Prohibition, was the third movie in which Cagney and Bogart co-starred. A fine cast and sharp direction rescued the hackneyed story involving army buddies in the aftermath of the first World War. Records reveal that ten contract writers worked on the script, supporting Cagney's complaint that the film was cranked out and depended upon the actors' ad-libbing to put heart in the script. There were a multitude of production problems: a succession of actresses were replaced for the role finally played by Gladys George; Raoul Walsh replaced director Anatole Litvak. One of Cagney's innovations was the "two for one" technique in a fight sequence: as a thug is slugged on the chin, his head snaps back to conk a second thug on the forehead. When the film opened to surprisingly good reviews and box office, everyone involved claimed credit for the success.

STARRING: James Cagney, Priscilla Lane, Humphrey Bogart, Gladys George
DIRECTOR: Raoul Walsh
EXECUTIVE PRODUCER: Hal. B. Wallis
SCREENPLAY: Jerry Wald, Richard MaCauley, Robert Rossen
Based on the original story by Mark Hellinger

OPPOSITE: *James Cagney, Humphrey Bogart*

THE WIZARD OF OZ

1 9 3 9 · M G M

Anecdotes about the film abound. The most memorable is L. B. Mayer's decision, after a first sneak preview, to remove the song "Over the Rainbow," which later won an Oscar for Arlen and Harburg and became Garland's signature song. W. C. Fields turned down the role of the Wizard; Fox wouldn't release Shirley Temple to play Dorothy; Buddy Ebson was originally signed for the Scarecrow; Gale Sondergaard was first choice as a beautiful and glamourous witch, until it was decided Margaret Hamilton should play her ugly.

Several sequences were dropped from the picture including "We're Out of the Woods," most of "Lions and Tigers and Bears," the music sequence of Dorothy's return to the Emerald City, and "The Jitter Bug," which cost $80,000 to make and took five weeks to shoot. Judy Garland was given a special Academy Award and Herbert Stothart won an Oscar for Best Original Score. A 1925 silent version had been made with Oliver Hardy.

STARRING: Judy Garland, Frank Morgan, Ray Bolger, Bert Lahr, Jack Haley, Billie Burke, Margaret Hamilton
DIRECTOR: Victor Fleming
PRODUCER: Mervyn Leroy
SCREENPLAY: Noel Langley, Florence Ryerson, Edgar Allan Woolf
ADAPTATION: Noel Langley
From the book by L. Frank Baum
MUSICAL ADAPTATION: Herbert Stothart
LYRICIST: E. Y. "Yip" Harburg
MUSIC: Harold Arlen

OPPOSITE: *Jack Haley, Ray Bolger, Judy Garland, Bert Lahr*

"If I only had some courage!" wailed the Cowardly Lion

with JUDY GARLAND
FRANK MORGAN
RAY BOLGER
BERT LAHR
JACK HALEY

THE WIZARD OF OZ

It's METRO-GOLDWYN-MAYER'S TECHNICOLOR TRIUMPH!

COUNTRY OF ORIGIN U. S. A.

WUTHERING HEIGHTS

1 9 3 9 • U n i t e d   A r t i s t s

Both Olivier and Oberon knew that they were not each others' choice for co-star and that knowledge didn't promote
a convivial working atmosphere between them. Olivier wanted Vivien Leigh (who turned down
the lesser role of Isabella) to play Cathy, and Oberon wanted Douglas Fairbanks Jr. (who had tested badly for the role)
as Heathcliff. Wyler was very anxious to have Olivier and courted him in England. Once in Hollywood, Olivier found Wyler to be a tyrant who disregarded his views on interpretation. During filming, Oberon twisted
her ankle in the heather and Olivier got athlete's foot from a pair of secondhand clogs; subsequent
scenes were played with one sitting and the other limping. Everyone fought against Goldwyn's tendency to glamourize
everything. He succeeded in updating the story thirty years because he preferred the more elaborate
fashions of the later period. Despite production problems, the movie earned good reviews and was nominated for eight
Academy Awards.

STARRING: Merle Oberon, Laurence Olivier, David Niven, Geraldine Fitzgerald, Flora Robson, Donald Crisp
DIRECTOR: William Wyler
PRODUCER: Samuel Goldwyn
Based on the novel by Emily Bronte
WRITERS: Ben Hecht and Charles MacArthur

OPPOSITE: *Left inset, Laurence Olivier, Miles Mander; center
cameo, Merle Oberon, Olivier; lower right inset,
Geraldine Fitzgerald*

"**I am Heathcliff**

I love a woman who belongs to another by law . . . My love was fierce . . . My hate is burning . . . *I will have vengeance!*"

SAMUEL GOLDWYN *presents*

WUTHERING HEIGHTS

A Story of Vengeful, Thwarted Love

co-starring **MERLE OBERON · LAURENCE OLIVIER · DAVID NIVEN**

with **Flora Robson** · Donald Crisp · Geraldine Fitzgerald · *Released thru* United Artists · *Directed by* **WILLIAM WYLER**

Screenplay by Ben Hecht and Charles MacArthur   *From the great novel by Emily Bronte*

THE LETTER

1 9 4 0 · W a r n e r   B r o s .

An earlier version of this film was made at Paramount in 1929 with Jeanne Eagles and Herbert Marshall; a later version, retitled *The Unfaithful*, was made in 1947. Bette Davis won a Best Actress nomination for her role as a planter's wife in Malaya who kills her lover, tries to evade prosecution and is eventually killed by her lover's wife (Gale Sondergaard). Director Wyler—known as "90-take Wyler"—worked so long on one particular scene that it's said he had shadows painted on the floor to match earlier lighting. His directing techniques required tremendous discipline from actors, many of whom were not accustomed to lengthy takes and resented his tyrannical perfectionism. The film was a success and earned an Oscar nomination for Best Picture.

STARRING: Bette Davis, Gale Sondergaard, Herbert Marshall
DIRECTOR: William Wyler
EXECUTIVE PRODUCER: Hal Wallis
SCREEN TREATMENT: Howard Koch
Based on the play by W. Somerset Maugham
COSTUMES: Orry-Kelly
MUSIC: Max Steiner

OPPOSITE: *Bette Davis*

BETTE DAVIS
The Letter
by W. SOMERSET MAUGHAM
with
HERBERT MARSHALL · JAMES STEPHENSON
FRIEDA INESCORT · GALE SONDERGAARD
A WILLIAM WYLER PRODUCTION
SCREEN PLAY BY HOWARD KOCH · MUSIC BY MAX STEINER · A WARNER BROS.-FIRST NATIONAL PICTURE
Presented by
WARNER BROS.
Country of Origin U. S. A.

MY LITTLE CHICKADEE

1940 · Universal

Joseph Calleia played the role originally offered to Humphrey Bogart, who abandoned the project because he was never given a completed script. Fields finished a first draft within a month but, heavy with pathos, it was given to Grover Jones to rewrite. The revisions appalled Fields, who dubbed the second draft "Corn With The Wind." Before filming commenced, West and Fields were in constant touch about the script. Nevertheless, West wrote her scenes, Fields wrote his; they collaborated on the rest. Once in front of the camera, West insisted on a line cut in one of Fields' scenes. She places a goat on her bed and leaves. Fields comes in, sits on the bed and sniffs. The offending dialogue: "Have you changed your cologne, dear?" She also objected to being referred to as "my little brood mare." Cordiality between the stars vanished and Cline stated, "I'm not directing, I'm refereeing." It was war on the set with both stars ad-libbing freely. Predictably, there were battles with the Hayes office. Fields lost the speech: "I know what I'll do. I'll go to India and become a missionary. I hear there's money in that, too." West's line to a card-player—"Is that a pistol in your pocket or are you just happy to see me?"—was spared. The movie got terrible notices, but eventually outgrossed every other Fields-Universal picture. Fields' reviews were good, infuriating West, who got a critical drubbing.

STARRING: Mae West, W. C. Fields, Joseph Calleia, Dick Foran, Margaret Hamilton
DIRECTOR: Eddie Cline
EXECUTIVE PRODUCER: Lester Cowan
PRODUCER: Jack Gross (uncredited)
ORIGINAL SCREENPLAY: Mae West and W. C. Fields
GOWNS: Vera West

OPPOSITE: *Mae West, Joseph Calleia, W. C. Fields*

MAE W.C.
WEST★FIELDS
in
My Little Chickadee

A NEW UNIVERSAL PICTURE

Copyright 1940 Universal Pictures Company, Inc. — Country of Origin U.S.A.

THE SEA HAWK

1 9 4 0 • W a r n e r   B r o s . / 1 s t   N a t i o n a l

This epic romantic adventure tale of the high seas shows the dashing Flynn at his finest. Originally intended as a remake of 1st National's 1924 version, only the title was retained. A new story line was based on Seton Miller's tale, "Beggars Of The Sea," supposedly about Sir Francis Drake. Warners used many of the sets, set dressings and costumes from Elizabeth and Essex, retaining a great deal of the lavish ($1,700,000) budget to inaugurate an enormous new sound stage. It housed two full-scale ships—one 165 feet long, another 135 feet long—both surrounded by 12 feet of water. Flynn gave up the habit of doing most of his own stunts, believing that Curtiz, who'd directed him in a number of other swashbucklers, had no respect for his safety.

Flora Robson reprised the role of Elizabeth I that she'd originally played in the 1937 British film *Fire Over England.*

STARRING: Errol Flynn, Brenda Marshall, Claude Rains, Alan Hale, Henry Daniell, Donald Crisp, Flora Robson
DIRECTOR: Michael Curtiz
EXECUTIVE PRODUCER: Hal B. Wallis
ASSOCIATE PRODUCER: Henry Blanke
ORIGINAL SCREENPLAY: Howard Koch, Seton I. Miller
MUSIC: Erich Wolfgang Korngold
COSTUMES: Orry-Kelly

OPPOSITE: *Henry Daniell, Errol Flynn*

ERROL FLYNN
THE SEA HAWK
Presented by
WARNER BROS.
Country of Origin U. S. A.

THEY DRIVE BY NIGHT

1 9 4 0 · W a r n e r B r o s

This story about truckers fighting their crooked bosses was a partial remake of *Bordertown*, a Bette Davis movie produced in 1935. Bogart plays Paul Fabrini who owns a trucking business with his brother (George Raft), and becomes crippled. A near-fatal filming accident occurred during a drive down a long hill in a beat-up truck. Raft was at the wheel, with Bogart and Sheridan as passengers, when the brakes failed. Their speed had hit 80 m.p.h. before Raft saw a bulldozer-break and was able to use the incline to stop his truck.

STARRING: George Raft, Ann Sheridan, Ida Lupino, Humphrey Bogart
DIRECTOR: Raoul Walsh
EXECUTIVE PRODUCER: Hal Wallis
ASSOCIATE PRODUCER: Mark Hellinger
SCREENPLAY: Jerry Wald, Richard Macaulay

OPPOSITE: *Humphrey Bogart, Ann Sheridan, George Raft*

CITIZEN KANE

1 9 4 1 · R K O

America was the working title for this brilliant expressionistic study of a millionaire newspaper magnate. Welles incarnated Kane and, at the age of 25, was given absolute authority over every aspect of the film.

It's disputed whether Welles or Mankiewicz came up with the idea for the Academy Award-winning screenplay, but it's certain that "Rosebud," the whispered reference to his childhood sled that Kane makes on his deathbed, was the inspiration of Mankiewicz. The picture penetrates deeply into the egotism and loneliness of the ruthless and universally feared Kane who uses his newspaper to foment war. William Randolph Hearst used his great personal influence and power, plus that of his newspaper empire, to prevent the release of this film that paralleled his life story. Though well received critically, the movie was not at the time understood or appreciated by audiences in general. Its commercial failure—along with the disastrous reception accorded Welles' *The Magnificent Ambersons* and *It's All True*—was instrumental in RKO's decision to drop him. *Citizen Kane* received the New York Film Critics Best Picture Award, the National Board of Review Best Picture, and was nominated for numerous Academy Awards, winning an Oscar only for the screenplay.

PRODUCED, DIRECTED AND STARRING: Orson Welles
WRITTEN BY: Orson Welles and Herman J. Mankiewicz
ASSOCIATE PRODUCER: Richard Baer

OPPOSITE: *Joseph Cotton, Orson Welles, Erskine Sanford, Everett Sloane*

It's Terrific!

ORSON WELLES
CITIZEN KANE

COUNTRY OF ORIGIN U. S. A. 4012/562

THE MALTESE FALCON

1 9 4 1 · W a r n e r   B r o s

Bogart plays Sam Spade in this classic thriller concerning the detective's search for a jewel-encrusted statue. George Raft had turned the role down, as he did Bogart's part in *High Sierra.* This was Huston's first directing assignment and the first of five films he did with Bogart. Greenstreet, an English-born stage actor, made his screen debut as the mysterious and ruthless Kasper Guttman. The bulky, 300-pound Greenstreet was subsequently teamed with the diminutive Lorre in several successful Warners' films. The novel had been filmed twice before, first in 1931 and again in 1936 as *Satan Met a Lady.* The movie, budgeted at only $300,000, was an instant favorite and met with critical acclaim.

STARRING: Humphrey Bogart, Mary Astor, Sydney Greenstreet, Peter Lorre, Elisha Cook Jr., Ward Bond
DIRECTOR: John Huston
EXECUTIVE PRODUCER: Hal Wallis
ASSOCIATE PRODUCER: Henry Blanke
SCREENPLAY: John Huston
Based on the story by Dashiell Hammett
PHOTOGRAPHY: Arthur Edeson

OPPOSITE: *Humphrey Bogart, Mary Astor*

HUMPHREY BOGART · MARY ASTOR

A
WARNER BROS.
FIRST NATIONAL
PICTURE

the Maltese Falcon

Country of Origin U.S.A.

SUSPICION

1 9 4 1 · R K O

An innocent young woman slowly comes to the realization that her husband is a murderer and plans to kill her, too.

In the novel, he does. Hitchcock planned to use that ending until RKO insisted that, while Grant's public might accept him as a petty swindler, they wouldn't believe him capable of murder. Hitchcock bitterly resented the compromise ending that begged the audience to believe that "the suspicion" was all a product of the wife's imagination. Critics, too, believed it spoiled a great picture. Joan Fontaine won an Oscar for Best Actress.

This was Grant's first picture with Hitchcock and the only Hitchcock/Grant film that was tampered with by the studio.

STARRING: Cary Grant, Joan Fontaine, Cedric Hardwicke, Nigel Bruce, Dame May Whitty
DIRECTOR: Alfred Hitchcock
SCREENPLAY: Samson Raphaelson, Joan Harrison and Alma Reville
From the novel "Before The Fact" by Frances Iles

OPPOSITE: *Joan Fontaine, Cary Grant*

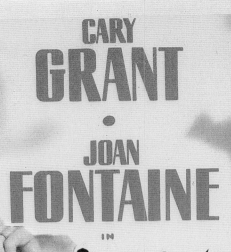

CARY
GRANT
•
JOAN
FONTAINE
in

Suspicion

with

SIR CEDRIC HARDWICKE
NIGEL BRUCE
DAME MAY WHITTY

R K O
RADIO
PICTURES

SHE WON YOUR HEART
IN "REBECCA"!

HE DREW YOUR CHEERS
IN "PHILADELPHIA STORY"

THRILL TO THEM TOGETHER
IN A SUSPENSE—ROMANCE
DIRECTED BY THE MAN
WHO DID "REBECCA"

ALFRED HITCHCOCK

Screen play by Samson Raphaelson, Joan Harrison, Alma Reville

41 316

WOMAN OF THE YEAR

1 9 4 2 · M G M

Hepburn plays Tess Harding, a political columnist, to Spencer Tracy's Sam Craig, a sportswriter for the same newspaper. They marry, but she neglects him in favor of her career. On the night she is given the
Woman of the Year Award, he leaves. Tess tries to become a dutiful housewife to win him back. Despite the best of
intentions, her efforts go awry and both realize she's not cut out for domestic chores. This was the
first pairing of Hepburn and Tracy, who were to do eight more films together, spanning a period of 28 years. When
they first met, the lanky Hepburn, wearing high heels, said, "I'm afraid I'm rather tall for you, Mr.
Tracy." He responded that he would soon cut her down to size. When Garson Kanin suggested to Tracy that he might
offer Hepburn first billing, he said: "Listen, chowderhead, a movie isn't a goddam lifeboat." Their
personal relationship would continue until the actor's death in 1967. The movie was a huge hit, provided Hepburn
with her fourth Academy Award nomination and won an Oscar for the screenplay.

STARRING: Spencer Tracy, Katharine Hepburn
DIRECTOR: George Stevens
PRODUCER: Joseph L. Mankiewicz
SCREENPLAY: Ring Lardner Jr., Michael Kanin

OPPOSITE: *Spencer Tracy, Katharine Hepburn*

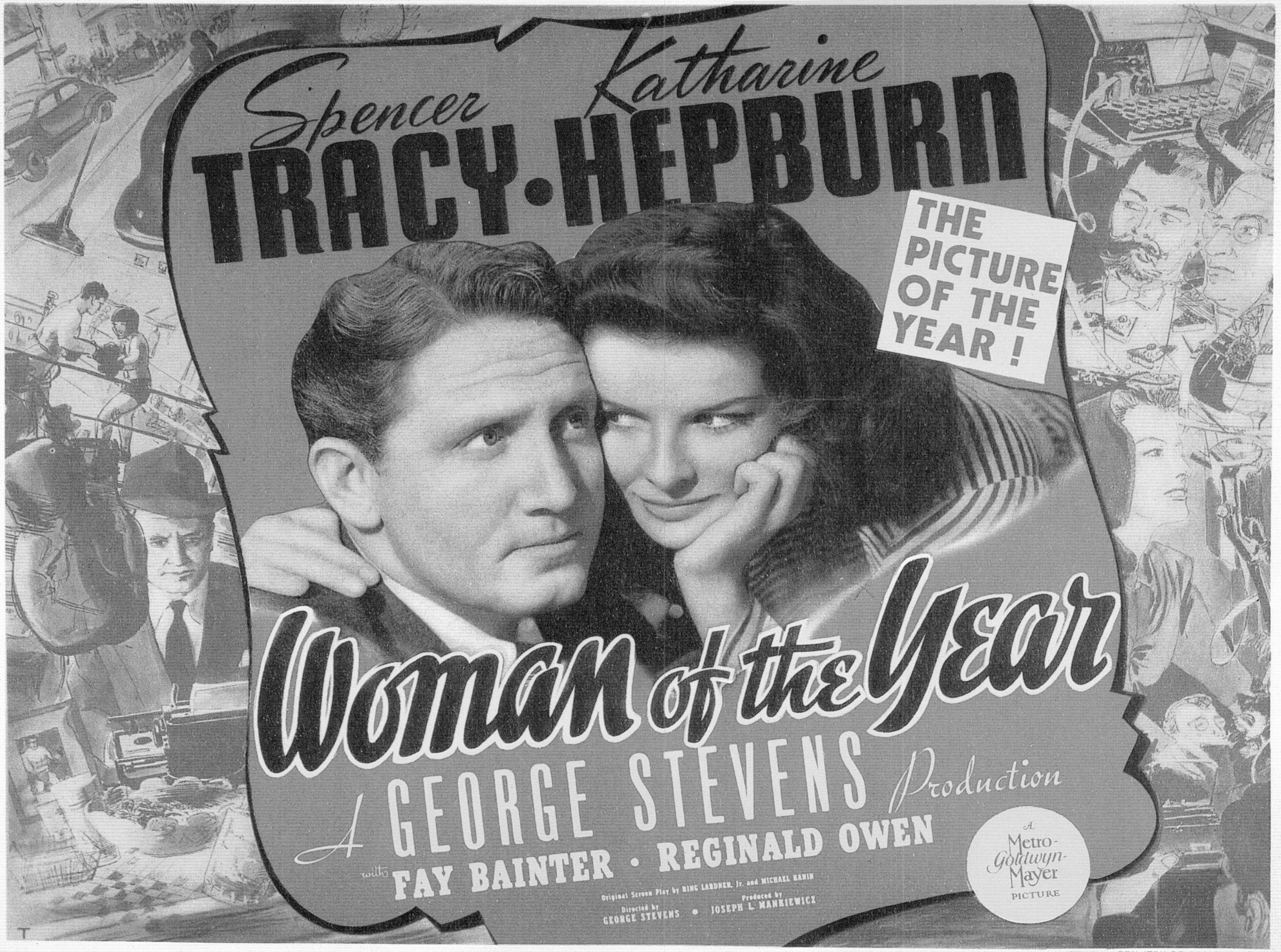

COUNTRY OF ORIGIN U. S. A.

YANKEE DOODLE DANDY

1 9 4 2 · W a r n e r   B r o s .

George M. Cohan's comment about himself—"Once a song and dance man, always a song and dance man"— also describes James Cagney, who portrayed him. This patriotic wartime homage started filming one day after the attack on Pearl Harbor. Cohan was terminally ill and in the last months of his life when he negotiated the rights to his life story, retaining cast and screenplay approval. He also stipulated that there could be no love scenes; however, Cagney reciting the song "Mary" to his bride plays as a tender love scene. Songs include "You're a Grand Old Flag," "Give My Regards To Broadway" and "Over There." On Broadway Cohan had produced 40 plays, helped finance 125 others and composed more than 500 songs; it was fitting that the film about this great showman should premiere in New York City. First-night-ticket sales from New York, London and Los Angeles reaped $5,750,000, providing funds for the purchase of three Liberty cargo vessels for the Atlantic Convoy. Cagney got great reviews and won an Academy Award for his performance.

STARRING: James Cagney, Walter Huston, Joan Leslie
DIRECTOR: Michael Curtiz
EXECUTIVE PRODUCER: Hal B. Wallis
PRODUCER: Jack L. Warner
ASSOCIATE PRODUCER: William Cagney
SCREENPLAY: Robert Buchner, Edmund Joseph
From the original story by Robert Buchner
CAMERAMAN: James Wong Howe

OPPOSITE: *Jeanne Cagney, James Cagney, Joan Leslie, Walter Huston (Uncle Sam) and Rosemary DeCamp (Liberty)*

James Cagney in "Yankee Doodle Dandy"

Based on the story of GEORGE M. COHAN

Presented by WARNER BROS. Pictures, Inc.

CASABLANCA

1 9 4 3 • W a r n e r   B r o s

In this great screen classic, Bogart plays Richard "Rick" Blaine, a stubborn, self-centered man of honor who becomes heroic by his refusal to compromise. Rick helps his old flame (Bergman) and her husband (Henreid), to escape from the Nazis in Vichy-controlled Casablanca. The release date, January 23, 1943, coincided with the Casablanca conference between Roosevelt and Churchill. Production was chaotic with pages hot off the typewriter handed to actors minutes before the scenes were to be filmed. "Actors! Actors! They want to know everything," said an exasperated Curtiz. No one knew whether Bergman would end up with nightclub-owner Rick or resistance leader Henreid. Two endings were written, but when the first was shot, they stayed with it. "Play it, Sam" and "Here's lookin' at you, kid" are two of of the most beloved lines from a Hollywood picture. The film was nominated for eight Oscars and won for Best Picture, Screenplay and Director.

STARRING: Humphrey Bogart, Ingrid Bergman, Paul Henreid, Peter Lorre, Conrad Veidt, Claude Rains,
Sydney Greenstreet, and Dooley Wilson as Sam, playing and singing "As Time Goes By"
DIRECTOR: Michael Curtiz
PRODUCER: Hal Wallis
SCREENPLAY: Julius J. Epstein, Philip G. Epstein, Howard Koch
Based on the unproduced play "Everybody Comes To Rick's" by Murray Burnett and Joan Allison
MUSIC: Max Steiner

OPPOSITE: *Peter Lorre, Humphrey Bogart*

A
WARNER
BROS.
PICTURE

CASABLANCA

Country of Origin U. S. A.

BIBLIOGRAPHY

ASTAIRE, Fred: *Fred Astaire*—Michael Freedland (W. H. Allen, 1976); *Fred Astaire*—Benny Green (Exeter Books, 1979); *The Fred Astaire and Ginger Rogers Book*—Arlene Croce (Outerbridge & Lazard, Inc., 1972)

ASTOR, Mary: *Mary Astor: A Life On Film*— (Delacorte Press, 1971)

BARRYMORE, John: *Damned in Paradise: The Life of John Barrymore*—John Kobler (Atheneum, 1977); *Good Night, Sweet Prince*—Gene Fowler (The Viking Press, 1944)

BENNETT, Joan: *The Bennett Playbill*—Joan Bennett and Lois Kibbee (Holt, Rinehart & Winston, 1970)

BOGART, Humphrey: *The Films of Humphrey Bogart*—Clifford McCarty (The Citadel Press, 1965); *Humphrey Bogart*—Nathaniel Benchley (Little, Brown & Co., 1975); *Humphrey Bogart*—Alan Frank (Exeter Books, 1982)

BOYER, Charles: *Charles Boyer: The Reluctant Lover*—Larry Swindell (Doubleday & Co., 1983)

CAGNEY, James: *Cagney: The Actor as Auteur*—Patrick McGilligan (A. S. Barnes & Co., 1975); *The Films of James Cagney*—Homer Dickens (The Citadel Press, 1972); *James Cagney: The Authorized Biography*—Doug Warren with James Cagney (St. Martin's Press, 1983); *James Cagney: A Celebration*—Richard Schickel (Little, Brown & Co., 1985); *James Cagney: In The Spotlight*—(Galley Press, 1980)

CHANEY, Lon: *Faces, Forms, Films: The Artistry of Lon Chaney*—Robert G. Anderson (A. S. Barnes & Co., 1971)

CHAPLIN, Charlie: *Chaplin's Films*—Uno Asplund (A. S. Barnes & Co., 1971); *Charles Chaplin*—Theodore Huff (Henry Schuman, 1951); *The Legend of Charlie Chaplin*—Peter Haining (W. H. Allen, 1982); *The Little Fellow: The Life and Work of Charles Spencer Chaplin*—Peter Cotes and Thelma Niklaus (Philosophical Library, 1951)

CHEVALIER, Maurice: *Chevalier*—Gene Ringgold and DeWitt Bodeen (The Citadel Press, 1973); *Maurice Chevlier*—Michael Freedland (Morrow & Co., Inc., 1981)

COLMAN, Ronald: *The Films of Ronald Colman*—Lawrence J. Quirk (The Citadel Press, 1977); *Ronald Colman: A Very Private Person*—Juliet Benita Colman

COOPER, Gary: *The Films of Gary Cooper*—Homer Dickens (The Citadel Press, 1970); *The Last Hero: A Biography of Gary Cooper*—Larry Swindell (Doubleday & Co., Inc., 1980)

DAVIS, Bette: *Bette Davis: Her Film and Stage Career*—Jeffrey Robinson (Proteus Reels, 1982); *Mother Goddamn*—Whitney Stine (Hawthorn Books, 1974)

De HAVILLAND, Olivia: *The Films of Olivia De Havilland*—Tony Thomas (The Citadel Press, 1983)

DeMILLE, Cecil B.: *DeMille: The Man and His Pictures*—Gabe Essoe and Raymond Lee (A. S.

Barnes & Co., 1970)

DIETRICH, Marlene: *The Films of Marlene Dietrich*—Homer Dickens (The Citadel Press, 1968); *Marlene: The Life of Marlene Dietrich*—Charles Higham (W. W. Norton & Co., 1977)

FAIRBANKS, Douglas: *Douglas Fairbanks: The Fourth Musketeer*—Ralph Hancock and Letitia Fairbanks (Henry Holt & Co., 1953); *The Fairbanks Album*—Douglas Fairbanks Jr. and Richard Schickel (Little, Brown & Co., 1975); *His Life In Pictures: A Speculation on Celebrity in America, Based on the Life of Douglas Fairbanks, Sr.*—Richard Schediel (Charterhouse, 1973); *His Majesty, The American: The Cinema of Douglas Fairbanks, Sr.*—John C. Tibbetts and James M. Welsh (A. S. Barnes & Co., 1977)

FAIRBANKS, Douglas, Jr.: *Knight Errant: A Biography of Douglas Fairbanks Jr.*—Brian Connell (Doubleday & Co., Inc., 1955)

FIELDS, W. C.: *W. C. Fields: A Life In Film*—Ronald J. Fields (St. Martin's Press, 1984)

FLYNN, Errol: *The Films of Errol Flynn*—Tony Thomas, Rudy Behlmer and Clifford McCarty (The Citadel Press, 1969); *My Wicked, Wicked Ways*—Errol Flynn (G. P. Putnams' Sons, 1959)

GABLE, Clark: *Dear Mr. G. — The Biography of Clark Gable*—Jean Garceau and Inez Cocke (Little, Brown & Co., 1961); *The Films of Clark Gable*—Gabe Essoe (The Citadel Press, 1970); *Long Live The King: A Biography of Clark Gable*—Lyn Tornabene (G. P. Putnams' Sons, 1976)

GARBO, Greta: *Garbo*—John Bainbridge (Holt, Rinehart & Winston, 1971); *Garbo*—Fritiof Billquist (G. P. Putnams' Sons, 1960); *Garbo: A Portrait*—Alexander Walker (MacMillan Publishing Co., Inc., 1980)

GISH, Lillian: *Dorothy & Lillian Gish*—Lillian Gish (Charles Scribner's Sons, 1973)

GRANT, Cary: *Cary Grant: A Celebration*—Richard Schickel (Little, Brown & Co., 1983); *Cary Grant: An Unauthorized Biography*—Albert Govoni (Henry Regnery Co., 1971); *Cary Grant: In The Spotlight*—(Galley Press, 1980); *The Films of Cary Grant*—Donald Deschner (The Citadel Press, 1973); *Haunted Idol: The Story of the Real Cary Grant*—Geoffrey Wansell (William Morrow & Co., 1984); *The Life and Loves of Cary Grant*—Lee Guthrie (Drake Publishers, Inc., 1977); *The Private Cary Grant*—William Currie McIntosh and William Weaver (Sidgwick & Jackson, 1983)

HARLOW, Jean: *The Films of Jean Harlow*—Michael Conway and Mark Ricci (The Citadel Press, 1965); *Jean Harlow*—Curtis F. Brown (Pyramid Publishing, 1977)

HEPBURN, Katharine: *The Films of Katharine Hepburn*—Homer Dickens (The Citadel Press, 1971); *Katharine Hepburn*—Sheridan Morley (Little, Brown & Co., 1984); *Katharine

Hepburn: Her Film and Stage Career*—Caroline Latham (Proteus Books, 1982)

KARLOFF, Boris: *Boris Karloff and His Films*—Paul M. Jensen (A. S. Barnes & Co., 1974)

KEATON, Buster: *Keaton*—Rudi Blesh (MacMillan Co., 1966); *Keaton: The Man Who Wouldn't Lie Down*—Tom Dardis (Charles Scribner's Sons, 1979)

LAUGHTON, Charles: *Charles Laughton: An Intimate Biography*—Charles Higham (Doubleday & Co., 1976); *The Laughton Story: An Intimate Story of Charles Laughton*—Kurt Singer (John C. Winston Co., 1954)

LAUREL & HARDY: *The Films of Laurel & Hardy*—William Everson (The Citadel Press, 1967); *Stan: The Life of Stan Laurel*—Fred Lawrence Guiles (Stein & Day, 1980)

LLOYD, Harold: *Harold Lloyd: The Shape of Laughter*—Richard Schickel (New York Graphic Society, 1974); *Harold Lloyd: The King of Daredevil Comedy*—Adam Reilly (McMillan Publishing Co., 1977)

LOMBARD, Carole: *The Films of Carole Lombard*—Frederick W. Ott (The Citadel Press, 1972); *Screwball: The Life of Carole Lombard*—Larry Swindell (William Morrow & Co., 1975)

LUGOSI, Bela: *Lugosi: The Man Behind The Cape*—Robert Cremer (Henry Regnery Co., 1976)

LUPINO, Ida: *Ida Lupino*—Jerry Vermilye (Pyramid, 1977)

MACDONALD, Jeanette: *The Films of Jeanette MacDonald and Nelson Eddy*—Eleanor Knowles (A. S. Barnes & Co., 1975); *The Jeanette MacDonald Story*—James Robert Parish (Mason/Charter, 1976)

MARX Brothers: *Hello, I Must Be Going: Groucho and His Friends*—Charlotte Chandler (Doubleday & Co., 1978); *Hooray For Captain Spaulding*—Richard Anobile (Crown Publishers, 1974); *The Marx Brothers at the Movies*—Paul D. Zimmerman and Burt Goldblatt (G. P. Putnams' Sons, 1968)

OBERON, Merle: *Princess Merle: The Romantic Life of Merle Oberon*—Charles Higham and Roy Moseley (Coward-McCann, Inc., 1983)

OLIVIER, Laurence: *Confessions of an Actor*—Laurence Olivier (Simon & Schuster, 1982); *Laurence Olivier: Theatre and Cinema*—Robert L. Daniels (A. S. Barnes & Co., 1980)

POWELL, William: *The Complete Films of William Powell*—Lawrence J. Quirk (The Citadel Press, 1986); *Gentleman: The William Powell Story*—Charles Francisco (St. Martin's Press, 1985)

RAFT, George: *George Raft*—Lewis Yablonsky (McGraw-Hill Book Co., 1974)

RATHBONE, Basil: *Basil Rathbone: His Life and His Films*—Michael B. Druxman (A. S. Barnes & Co., 1975)

STEWART, James: *Everybody's Man: A Biography of James Stewart*—Jhan Robbins (G. P.

Putnams' Sons, 1985); *The Films of James Stewart*—Ken D. Jones, Arthur F. McClure and Alfred E. Twombley (A. S. Barnes & Co., 1970); *James Stewart*—Allen Eyles (Stein & Day, 1984); *James Stewart*—Allan Hunter (Spellmount Ltd., 1985)

SWANSON, Gloria: *The Films of Gloria Swanson*—Lawrence J. Quirk (The Citadel Press, 1984); *Swanson on Swanson*—Gloria Swanson (Random House, 1980)

TEMPLE, Shirley: *The Shirley Temple Story*—Lester and Irene David (G. P. Putnams' Sons, 1983)

VALENTINO, Rudolph: *The Magic of Rudolph Valentino*—Norman MacKenzie (The Research Publishing Co., 1970); *Valentino*—Irving Shulman (Trident Press, 1967)

WEST, Mae: *The Films of Mae West*—John Tuska (The Citadel Press, 1973)

American Silent Film—William K. Everson (Oxford University Press, 1978)

An Illustrated History of the Horror Film—Carlos Clarens (G. P. Putnams' Sons, 1967)

Born to Lose: The Gangster Film in America—Eugene Rosow (Oxford University Press, 1978)

Classics of the Horror Film—William K. Everson (The Citadel Press, 1974)

Classics of the Gangster Film—Robert Bookbinder (The Citadel Press, 1985)

Classic Movie Monsters—Donald Glut (Scarecrow Press, 1978)

Crime Movies: From Griffith to the Godfather and Beyond—Carlos Clarens (W. W. Norton & Co., 1980)

Dance in the Hollywood Musical—Jerome Delamater (UMI Research Press, 1981)

Dictionary of Film Makers—Georges Sadoul (University of California Press, 1972)

Dictionary of Films—Georges Sadoul (University of California Press, 1965)

The Film Encyclopedia—Ephraim Katz (The Putnam Publishing Group, 1979)

The Hollywood Musical—Ethan Mordden (St. Martin's Press, 1981)

The Horror People—John Brosnan (St. Martin's Press, 1976)

The Making of Citizen Kane—Robert L. Carringer (University of California Press, 1985)

The Making of King Kong—Orville Goldner and George E. Turner (A. S. Barnes & Co., 1975)

The Making of the Wizard of Oz—Aljean Harmetz (Alfred A. Knopf, 1977)

Movies of the Silent Years—Ann Lloyd (Orbis Publishing, 1984)

Movies of the Thirties—Ann Lloyd (Orbis Publishing, 1983)

TV, Movies and Video Guide (1987 Edition)—Leonard Maltin (New American Library, 1986)